The Muse Within

Exploring Creativity, Preference, and Cultural Evolution

By

Behzad Ghorbani

Copyright © 2024 by Behzad Ghorbani

All rights reserved. No part of this book may be reproduced, distributed, or transmitted in any form or by any means, including photocopying, recording, or other electronic or mechanical methods, without the prior written permission of the publisher, except in the case of brief quotations embodied in critical reviews and certain other non-commercial uses permitted by copyright law. This book is independently published by the author through Amazon Kindle Direct Publishing (KDP).

First Edition

Published by Amazon.com

10 9 8 7 6 5 4 3 2 1

November 2024

ISBN: 9798300205669

Cover Design by Amazon

CONTENTS

1	The Recursive Mind and the Art of Discovery	8
2	The Role of the Autonomic Nervous System	13
3	The Cultural Mirror: Discoveries, Art, and the Shaping of Collective Taste	18
4	Impressionism and the Train	24
5	Cubism and X-Rays	28
6	Surrealism and Psychoanalysis	33
7	Abstract Expressionism and the Atomic Bomb	38
8	Pop Art and Mass Media	42
9	Minimalism and Industrial Design	47
10	Digital Art and the Internet	52
11	Why We Like What We Like	57
12	Why We Dislike What We Dislike	62
13	The Role of Memory and Emotion	67
14	From Aversion to Appreciation	72

15	The Next Wave of Creativity	77
16	How to Expand What We Like	82
17	The Role of Discovery in Shaping New Tastes	87
18	Predicting Future Movements	92
19	Designing for the Mind	96
20	Conclusion: The Recursive Muse of Humanity	101
	Bibliography	105
	References	110

Chapter 1: The Recursive Mind and the Art of Discovery

Human creativity has always been driven by the need to make sense of the world, to interpret its patterns, and to transform those patterns into something meaningful. This process, far from being straightforward or linear, is deeply recursive. The human brain does not merely absorb information, it mirrors, refines, and reinterprets it, creating layers of understanding that unfold over time. This recursive nature is the bedrock of human thought, and it underpins not only our capacity to innovate but also our deeply personal responses to the things we love and the things we reject.

The concept of recursion is both elegant and profound. At its core, recursion involves taking a piece of information and looping it back upon itself, refining and reprocessing it with each iteration. In the brain, this occurs on multiple levels. Sensory inputs from the world, images, sounds, textures, are mirrored across the hemispheres, creating a dynamic interplay that allows us to construct coherent perceptions of reality. Patterns of light, for instance, are first broken down into their simplest components, shapes, colours, and contrasts, before being reassembled into the complex images we see.

But the brain's recursive abilities extend beyond perception. They allow us to reflect on our thoughts, to imagine possibilities, and to engage in the abstract reasoning that gives rise to art, science, and philosophy. It is this recursive interplay that transforms a fleeting observation into a work of art or a scientific breakthrough. When Einstein described time and space as relative, or when Monet painted the shimmer of sunlight on water, they were engaging in the same recursive process, taking what they saw, reflecting on it, and refining it into something new.

At the same time, our experiences of art, discovery, and creativity are not purely cerebral. They are deeply tied to the autonomic nervous system (ANS), which governs our physiological responses to the world. The ANS operates in two modes: the sympathetic system, which drives arousal and excitement, and the parasympathetic system, which promotes relaxation and calm. Together, these systems create the ebb and flow of our emotional and physical states, shaping how we respond to the stimuli around us.

When we encounter something new, an unfamiliar piece of art, an innovative idea, or a sudden realisation, the sympathetic system often takes the lead. Our heart rate quickens, our pupils dilate, and we feel a surge of energy. This heightened state of arousal primes the brain to focus, to engage deeply with the novel stimulus. But for us to truly appreciate and integrate what we've encountered, the parasympathetic system must follow, allowing us to process and reflect. This oscillation between arousal and relaxation is at the heart of how we form preferences, whether for a type of music, a work of art, or a new scientific paradigm.

This interplay between the brain and the body becomes particularly evident when we consider the history of human discoveries and their impact on art and culture. Inventions like the train, the camera, and the X-ray did not just change the way people lived; they transformed the way they saw the world. These technological advances introduced new patterns, new ways of perceiving time, space, and motion. Artists, in turn, mirrored these patterns in their work, creating movements like Impressionism, Cubism, and Surrealism that captured the shifting landscapes of human experience.

The train, for instance, was not merely a mode of transport but a new way of experiencing motion. It transformed the landscape into a blur of fleeting impressions, a dynamic interplay of light and colour. Artists like Monet and Degas mirrored these sensations in their work, breaking away from the rigid realism of the past to embrace the ephemeral beauty of the moment. Similarly, the camera revolutionised the way people thought about time and perspective, inspiring painters to experiment with composition and photographers to capture the world in ways never before possible.

Each of these artistic movements reflects the recursive processes of the brain, which seeks to integrate the unfamiliar into the familiar, the chaotic into the ordered. The fractured perspectives of Cubism, for example, mimic the brain's ability to deconstruct and reconstruct reality, while the dreamlike imagery of Surrealism mirrors the recursive loops of thought that occur in the unconscious mind. These art forms are not merely products of their time; they are mirrors of the human mind itself.

But what determines whether we find these movements compelling or alienating? Why do some people love the bold, chaotic lines of Abstract Expressionism, while others are drawn to the serene landscapes of the Renaissance? The answer lies in the unique interplay between each individual's cerebral patterns, shaped by their experiences and culture, and their autonomic nervous system, which colours every encounter with a physiological response.

When we look at a painting or hear a piece of music, our brains immediately begin to mirror its patterns, comparing them to the patterns we have already stored. If the artwork aligns with our expectations while offering just enough novelty to surprise us, we feel a sense of delight. If it challenges our patterns too much, or not at all, the response may be discomfort or boredom. At the same time, our ANS responds to the artwork's colours, textures, and rhythms, creating a visceral reaction that amplifies or tempers our cerebral engagement.

This dynamic interplay of brain, body, and culture is what makes human creativity so rich and multifaceted. It is why each era produces its own distinctive art, shaped by the discoveries and inventions of the time, and why each individual's preferences are as unique as their experiences. To understand why we like what we like, we must look not only at the art itself but also at the intricate web of patterns, emotions, and cultural narratives that connect it to our minds.

As we explore the relationship between discovery and creativity in the chapters ahead, we will see how each invention, from the train to the atomic bomb, has not only changed the world but also reshaped the way we perceive and create. These shifts are not merely historical; they are deeply personal, woven into the fabric of how we think, feel, and respond. In the recursive mirror of art and invention, we see ourselves reflected, our desires, our fears, and our endless capacity to reimagine the world.

Chapter 2: The Role of the Autonomic Nervous System

While much of human creativity and preference can be attributed to the recursive processes of the mind, the experience of liking or disliking something is deeply rooted in the body. The **autonomic nervous system (ANS)**, the network responsible for regulating involuntary bodily functions, plays an integral role in shaping our emotional and aesthetic responses. Its silent orchestration of arousal and relaxation creates the physical sensations that accompany our encounters with art, music, literature, and even everyday objects.

The ANS operates through two primary branches: the **sympathetic nervous system (SNS)** and the **parasympathetic nervous system (PNS)**. These two systems work in tandem to create a dynamic balance between excitement and calm. The SNS is often described as the body's accelerator. It governs the fight-or-flight response, increasing heart rate, dilating pupils, and preparing the body for action when we encounter something novel, exciting, or threatening. In contrast, the PNS functions as the brake, restoring balance by slowing the heart rate, promoting digestion, and encouraging rest and reflection.

When we engage with art or other forms of creativity, the interaction between these systems shapes our experience. Imagine encountering an unfamiliar painting in a gallery. The vibrant colours, bold lines, or unusual composition might initially trigger the SNS, producing a surge of arousal. You might feel your heart rate quicken slightly or experience a heightened focus as your brain tries to make sense of the unfamiliar. But as you gaze longer, the PNS begins to take over, allowing you to relax into the piece and absorb its subtleties. This ebb and flow of nervous system activity underpins the rich tapestry of human aesthetic experience.

The key to understanding why we find certain forms of art engaging lies in the **oscillation** between these two states. Art that overstimulates the SNS, perhaps through chaotic, dissonant patterns, can feel overwhelming, while art that overly engages the PNS, through monotony or excessive simplicity, may be dismissed as dull. The most captivating works strike a balance, engaging both systems to create an interplay of tension and resolution. This dynamic mirrors the brain's recursive loops, where patterns are continually refined and integrated.

The Impressionist movement, for example, embodies this balance. Paintings like Monet's *Water Lilies* or Renoir's *Dance at Le Moulin de la Galette* offer a delicate harmony of stimulation and tranquillity. The shimmering light and vivid colours activate the SNS, drawing the viewer in, while the gentle brushstrokes and fluid compositions engage the PNS, fostering a sense of calm. This dual activation creates a state of **relaxed engagement**, allowing the viewer to feel both energised and soothed.

On the other hand, movements like Abstract Expressionism, exemplified by Jackson Pollock's chaotic drip paintings, often tip the balance toward sympathetic activation. The seemingly random splashes of paint, the frenetic energy of the composition, and the scale of the works bombard the senses, creating an experience that can feel exhilarating or unsettling, depending on the viewer's tolerance for stimulation. For some, this heightened arousal leads to a sense of catharsis, as the sympathetic response eventually gives way to the calming influence of the parasympathetic system. For others, the lack of resolution leaves them feeling restless or disconnected.

The physiological interplay of the ANS also explains why certain forms of art are more appealing in specific contexts. Minimalism, with its clean lines and muted tones, often resonates in environments where overstimulation is the norm. A minimalist sculpture by Donald Judd or a serene Rothko canvas can offer a counterbalance to the frenetic pace of modern life, engaging the parasympathetic system and providing a moment of calm in an otherwise chaotic world.

But the role of the ANS in shaping our preferences goes beyond the immediate experience of art. It also governs how we process memories and emotions, both of which play a crucial role in determining what we like or dislike. When we encounter something that evokes a positive emotional memory, the parasympathetic system is likely to be activated, reinforcing our attachment to that stimulus. A song that reminds us of a joyful moment, for instance, may produce a sense of warmth and relaxation. Conversely, stimuli associated with negative memories are more likely to trigger a sympathetic response, creating discomfort or aversion.

This connection between the ANS and memory is particularly evident in the way cultural and historical experiences shape collective preferences. The Romantic movement, for example, arose during a period of rapid industrialisation and urbanisation, when the noise and chaos of cities were overwhelming the senses. The Romantic focus on sublime landscapes and emotional depth offered a parasympathetic counterbalance, appealing to an audience yearning for escape and introspection. Similarly, the stark, ordered aesthetic of Bauhaus design reflected the need for clarity and simplicity in a world recovering from the disarray of war.

As we move further into the modern age, the ANS continues to adapt to new forms of sensory and emotional input. Digital art, with its interactive and immersive qualities, engages both systems simultaneously. A virtual reality experience, for example, might stimulate the sympathetic system through its novelty and vividness while activating the parasympathetic system through its meditative, exploratory nature. This dual engagement mirrors the recursive loops of the brain, creating a deeply immersive experience that feels both energising and grounding.

Understanding the role of the ANS in shaping our aesthetic responses allows us to appreciate the deeply embodied nature of creativity. Liking or disliking something is not merely a matter of intellectual judgement; it is a visceral process, rooted in the rhythms of our nervous system. The interplay between the brain's cognitive patterns and the body's physiological responses creates a dynamic, evolving relationship with the art, ideas, and experiences we encounter.

As we explore the connections between human discoveries and artistic movements in the chapters ahead, the ANS will remain a central thread, highlighting how inventions not only change the way we think but also the way we feel. Whether it is the soothing rhythms of Impressionism, the stimulating chaos of Abstract Expressionism, or the balanced harmony of digital art, our preferences are shaped by the intricate dance of arousal and relaxation, stimulation and resolution. In this dance, we find the essence of what it means to engage with the world, to like, to dislike, and ultimately, to create.

Chapter 3: The Cultural Mirror: Discoveries, Art, and the Shaping of Collective Taste

Human creativity thrives at the intersection of invention and imagination. While individual cognition and physiology play crucial roles in shaping preferences, it is within the cultural sphere that discoveries and artistic movements find their deepest resonance. Each era brings with it transformative innovations, trains, cameras, X-rays, psychoanalysis, that redefine how societies perceive time, space, and reality itself. These shifts ripple through the collective consciousness, shaping artistic expression and altering what people find beautiful, meaningful, or intriguing.

The relationship between discovery and art is reciprocal. Just as inventions inspire new artistic movements, these movements, in turn, shape how societies understand and assimilate the inventions themselves. This interplay can be seen throughout history, as discoveries challenge existing paradigms and compel artists to reimagine the world in ways that align with, or critique, these changes. To explore this dynamic is to trace the evolving relationship between culture, technology, and creativity, revealing the intricate web of influence that binds them together.

One of the clearest examples of this interplay can be found in the 19th century, when the Industrial Revolution reshaped nearly every aspect of daily life. Factories, railroads, and urbanisation created a world of unprecedented motion and mechanisation, altering how people experienced space and time. This rapid transformation gave rise to the Romantic movement, which offered a counterbalance to the era's technological fervour. Romantic artists like J. M. W. Turner and Caspar David Friedrich turned their gaze to sublime landscapes, capturing the awe-inspiring power of nature. Their works resonated deeply with audiences seeking respite from the relentless pace of industrial progress.

Yet even within this Romantic yearning for nature, the influence of technology was unmistakable. Turner's famous painting *Rain, Steam, and Speed – The Great Western Railway* depicted a train hurtling through the countryside, its smoke blending with the clouds and mist. The painting captured the paradoxical relationship between nature and industry, presenting the train as both a marvel of human ingenuity and an intrusion into the pastoral landscape. Turner's work mirrored the cultural ambivalence of his time, reflecting a society simultaneously enamoured with and wary of its own creations.

This pattern, the emergence of art movements as responses to cultural and technological change, continued into the 20th century, when discoveries like X-rays and psychoanalysis redefined how people understood reality. X-rays revealed hidden structures within the human body, challenging traditional notions of surface and solidity. Artists like Pablo Picasso and Georges Braque, inspired by this new way of seeing, developed Cubism, a movement that fragmented objects into geometric planes. Cubist works invited viewers to consider multiple perspectives simultaneously, mirroring the disjointed yet interconnected nature of modern life.

Psychoanalysis, pioneered by Sigmund Freud, offered a different kind of revelation, one that delved into the hidden recesses of the mind. Freud's exploration of the unconscious inspired the Surrealist movement, which sought to depict the dreamlike and the irrational. Artists like Salvador Dalí and René Magritte created works that juxtaposed ordinary objects in extraordinary ways, challenging viewers to question their assumptions about reality. Surrealism resonated with a world grappling with the aftermath of war and the fragility of rationality, offering a window into the subconscious that mirrored the introspective mood of the time.

What makes these movements so compelling is their ability to reflect and amplify the cultural narratives of their eras. Art, in this sense, acts as a cultural mirror, capturing the anxieties, aspirations, and contradictions of society. The train in Turner's painting, the fragmented forms in Picasso's *Les Demoiselles d'Avignon*, and the melting clocks in Dalí's *The Persistence of Memory* are not just artistic choices; they are cultural artefacts, shaped by and shaping the way people thought about the world.

But this mirroring is not passive. Art movements often challenge cultural narratives, offering new ways of seeing that disrupt the status quo. Impressionism, for example, emerged as a rebellion against the academic traditions of the Salon, which favoured detailed realism and historical themes. By focusing on everyday scenes and transient effects of light, Impressionist artists invited viewers to reconsider what was worthy of artistic representation. Their work resonated with a society increasingly shaped by the fleeting rhythms of modern life, from the rapid motion of trains to the ephemeral glow of gas lamps.

The reciprocal relationship between art and culture extends to the way artistic movements influence collective taste. Once marginalised or controversial, many movements eventually become mainstream, shaping the preferences of future generations. The Impressionists, initially dismissed as radicals, are now celebrated as masters, their works adorning the walls of major museums and influencing contemporary artists. This evolution reflects the brain's recursive capacity to adapt to and integrate new patterns, as well as the role of cultural exposure in expanding collective taste.

Cultural exposure is a powerful force, shaping not only what we like but also how we interpret the world. The ubiquity of television in the mid-20th century, for instance, created a shared visual language that Pop Art both embraced and critiqued. Artists like Andy Warhol and Roy Lichtenstein used the imagery of consumer culture, soup cans, comic strips, advertisements, to create works that resonated with a mass audience. By mirroring the aesthetics of mass production, Pop Art blurred the lines between high and low culture, challenging traditional notions of artistic value.

The influence of cultural exposure is not limited to visual art. Music, fashion, and design all reflect the interplay between invention and taste, shaping and being shaped by the cultural moment. The rise of electronic music, for example, was inseparable from the development of synthesisers and digital technology. Similarly, the minimalist aesthetic of Bauhaus design reflected the streamlined efficiency of industrialisation, influencing everything from architecture to typography.

As we explore these connections, it becomes clear that the cultural mirror is not a static reflection but a dynamic interplay of influence and adaptation. Each new discovery introduces patterns that ripple through society, reshaping art, preferences, and collective identity. These patterns, in turn, become the building blocks of future innovations, creating a recursive loop that defines the evolution of creativity.

Understanding this dynamic allows us to see art not as a fixed product but as an ongoing dialogue between the individual, the collective, and the technological. Whether it is the swirling steam in Turner's railway paintings, the fragmented forms of Cubism, or the ironic imagery of Pop Art, each movement tells a story of its time, a story of invention, adaptation, and the endless capacity of the human mind to reimagine the world.

Chapter 4: Impressionism and the Train

The invention of the train in the nineteenth century brought with it a profound transformation in how humans experienced time, space, and movement. For centuries, travel had been tied to the rhythms of the natural world, dictated by the steady pace of walking, horseback riding, or sailing. Journeys were laborious, unfolding slowly, allowing landscapes to emerge gradually. The train changed everything. It introduced speed and fluidity, enabling people to traverse vast distances in a fraction of the time they once required. This new mode of travel altered not only physical mobility but also human perception itself.

For the first time, landscapes were not walked upon or observed from a stationary vantage point but were seen rushing past at extraordinary speeds. The world became a blur of shifting colours and shapes, fragmented and fleeting. The scene you gazed at seconds ago no longer existed, replaced by another equally transient view. This phenomenon, novel and disorienting, profoundly influenced the way people thought about motion, time, and the relationship between the observer and the observed. Among those most affected by this new experience were the artists of the Impressionist movement, who sought to capture the essence of a world in constant flux.

Impressionism emerged as a radical departure from the rigid, detailed realism that had dominated European art for centuries. Instead of striving to depict reality with painstaking accuracy, Impressionist painters focused on capturing the fleeting impressions of light, colour, and atmosphere. The movement was defined by its loose, visible brushstrokes and its emphasis on moments of everyday life. Yet beneath its seemingly simple approach lay a sophisticated response to the changing world brought about by industrialisation and technological advancement. The train, in particular, played a crucial role in shaping the aesthetic principles of Impressionism.

Claude Monet, one of the leading figures of the movement, exemplified this new approach in works like *Impression, Sunrise*. In this painting, Monet depicted the harbour of Le Havre at sunrise, focusing not on fine details but on the play of light and colour. The reflections on the water, the soft haze of the morning, and the faint silhouettes of boats and industrial structures all combined to create a scene that felt alive and immediate. This painting, which lent its name to the entire movement, was not a representation of reality as it was but as it felt in a single, transient moment.

The experience of train travel was deeply embedded in the consciousness of Impressionist artists. For them, the train station became a symbol of modernity, a microcosm of the industrial age. Monet's series of paintings depicting the Gare Saint-Lazare in Paris captured the energy and dynamism of these spaces. The swirling steam from locomotives mixed with light and shadow, creating an interplay of movement and stillness that mirrored the sensations of the train journey itself. The station was both a place of arrival and departure, a liminal space where time seemed to stretch and compress in ways that reflected the larger transformations of the era.

The brain's response to these new sensory experiences offers insight into why Impressionism resonated so deeply with both its creators and its audience. The train's rapid motion presented a fragmented view of the world, challenging the brain's ability to process and integrate visual information. The recursive nature of human cognition, the brain's capacity to mirror, reflect, and refine sensory inputs, became crucial in adapting to this new way of seeing. Impressionist art mirrored this cognitive process, breaking down scenes into their essential elements and allowing the viewer to reconstruct them in their mind.

The autonomic nervous system also played a role in shaping the emotional responses to Impressionist works. The sympathetic nervous system, activated during moments of excitement or novelty, was likely engaged during train travel, as passengers experienced the thrill and disorientation of high-speed motion. Impressionist paintings, with their vibrant colours and dynamic compositions, stimulated similar feelings of energy and immediacy. At the same time, the parasympathetic nervous system, responsible for calming the body, was engaged by the soothing rhythms of Impressionist brushstrokes and the gentle, harmonious interplay of light and shadow. This dual activation of arousal and relaxation created a balanced emotional response that made Impressionist art both stimulating and comforting.

Impressionism also reflected a deeper cultural yearning for simplicity and connection with nature. In a world increasingly dominated by factories, machines, and urban sprawl, the Impressionists turned their gaze to gardens, rivers, and rural landscapes. Yet even these natural scenes were infused with the awareness of impermanence. The dappled light filtering through trees, the ripples on the surface of a pond, and the fleeting expressions of human figures all captured the transient beauty of the moment. This sensibility resonated with audiences who were themselves grappling with the pace of change in their lives.

The legacy of Impressionism extends far beyond its immediate historical context. Its emphasis on light, colour, and movement laid the groundwork for numerous artistic innovations in the twentieth century, from the bold experiments of the Fauves to the abstract explorations of modernist painters. Impressionism also anticipated the fragmented visual language of photography and film, media that would come to define the modern era. In many ways, the train not only transformed the physical landscape but also set in motion a chain of cultural and artistic shifts that continue to shape how we see the world today.

Through Impressionism, we gain a window into the profound interplay between technology, perception, and art. The train, as a symbol of modernity, became more than a machine; it became a catalyst for reimagining reality itself. In the hands of Monet, Degas, and their contemporaries, the fleeting views from a train window were transformed into a new way of seeing, a way that embraced the transient, the ephemeral, and the beautifully imperfect.

Chapter 5: Cubism and X-Rays

The early twentieth century was a time of profound transformation. Advances in science and technology were reshaping the way people understood the world, revealing layers of reality that had long been hidden from view. Among these breakthroughs, the discovery of X-rays in 1895 stood out as a moment of awe and disorientation. For the first time, human beings could look beneath the surface of solid objects, glimpsing the skeletal structures that lay hidden within. This revelation had implications far beyond medicine, influencing art, literature, and philosophy in ways that continue to resonate.

The idea that reality could be deconstructed and reimagined found its most striking expression in the artistic movement known as Cubism. Led by Pablo Picasso and Georges Braque, Cubism shattered the conventions of perspective and representation that had dominated Western art for centuries. Objects were no longer depicted as fixed, unified forms but as fragmented planes and overlapping perspectives. This radical approach mirrored the way X-rays revealed multiple layers of an object simultaneously, challenging the notion of a singular, coherent reality.

The connection between X-rays and Cubism was not merely conceptual; it was deeply rooted in the changing visual culture of the time. As X-ray images began to circulate in scientific and popular media, they introduced a new way of seeing, one that emphasised transparency, fragmentation, and multiplicity. These images disrupted the traditional distinction between interior and exterior, forcing viewers to consider the complex structures underlying the visible world. Cubist artists internalised this perspective, using their canvases to explore the hidden geometries of reality.

One of the most iconic works of early Cubism, Picasso's *Les Demoiselles d'Avignon* (1907), exemplifies this approach. The painting depicts five women, their bodies fractured into sharp, angular planes. Their faces, influenced by African masks, reject the naturalistic representation of human features, instead presenting a stylised, almost abstract vision. The figures appear simultaneously flat and dimensional, as if Picasso were trying to capture not just their outward appearance but the essence of their form from multiple angles. This technique reflects the influence of X-ray imagery, which similarly collapses the boundaries between inside and outside, front and back.

Braque, Picasso's close collaborator, took this exploration even further in works like *Violin and Candlestick* (1910). Here, the violin, a symbol of harmony and tradition, is deconstructed into a series of interlocking shapes. The candlestick, once a symbol of light and clarity, becomes a fragmented abstraction. The viewer is invited to reconstruct these objects mentally, piecing together their fragmented forms into a coherent whole. This process mirrors the brain's recursive capacity to integrate disjointed visual inputs, a process that was becoming increasingly relevant in a world shaped by new technologies and perspectives.

The cognitive engagement required by Cubism is one of the reasons it remains so compelling, and, for some, so challenging. Unlike traditional art, which offers a clear and unified representation of its subject, Cubist works demand active participation from the viewer. The brain must mirror the fragmented forms, reflect on their possible meanings, and refine its interpretation over time. This recursive engagement mirrors the process by which the brain interprets complex sensory inputs in daily life, making Cubism a deeply psychological art form.

Physiologically, Cubism engages the autonomic nervous system in a dynamic way. The initial encounter with a Cubist painting often triggers sympathetic activation. The fragmented forms, unusual angles, and lack of immediate recognisability create a sense of disorientation, stimulating arousal and curiosity. As the viewer spends more time with the painting, the parasympathetic system begins to assert itself, allowing for reflection and deeper understanding. This oscillation between arousal and relaxation creates a sense of intellectual and emotional satisfaction, making the experience of Cubism both stimulating and rewarding.

The cultural context in which Cubism emerged also shaped its aesthetic and philosophical underpinnings. The early twentieth century was marked by rapid technological and scientific advancements, from the invention of the aeroplane to the development of quantum mechanics. These breakthroughs challenged traditional ways of thinking about time, space, and causality, introducing new paradigms that emphasised complexity and uncertainty. Cubism reflected these shifts, offering a visual language that embraced fragmentation and multiplicity as fundamental aspects of reality.

The influence of Cubism extended far beyond the canvas. In architecture, figures like Le Corbusier drew inspiration from Cubist principles, designing buildings that emphasised geometric forms and functional transparency. In literature, writers like Gertrude Stein adopted a Cubist approach to language, using repetition and fragmented syntax to capture the rhythms of modern life. Even music felt the impact, with composers like Igor Stravinsky experimenting with dissonance and overlapping motifs to create compositions that echoed the visual complexity of Cubist art.

But perhaps the most profound legacy of Cubism lies in its ability to challenge and expand the boundaries of perception. By breaking objects into fragments and presenting multiple perspectives simultaneously, Cubism forced viewers to reconsider the nature of reality itself. It invited them to see the world not as a fixed and static entity but as a dynamic interplay of forms, angles, and dimensions. This perspective, once radical, has become increasingly relevant in a world shaped by digital technology, where reality is constantly deconstructed and reconstructed through screens, algorithms, and virtual environments.

Cubism's connection to X-rays is more than a historical curiosity; it is a testament to the power of human creativity to adapt and respond to new ways of seeing. Just as X-rays revealed the hidden structures of the body, Cubism revealed the hidden structures of thought and perception, offering a visual language that continues to resonate in the modern era. Through its fragmented planes and overlapping perspectives, Cubism reminds us that reality is always more complex than it appears, and that the act of seeing is, itself, a creative endeavour.

Chapter 6: Surrealism and Psychoanalysis

The early twentieth century was a time of profound introspection, a period when science turned inward to explore the most enigmatic terrain of all: the human mind. With Sigmund Freud at the forefront, psychoanalysis revealed that much of human behaviour and thought was governed not by rational decision-making but by the unconscious, a hidden world of desires, fears, and memories. This revelation fundamentally changed how people understood themselves and their place in the world. It also inspired a group of artists and writers who sought to bridge the gap between conscious and unconscious experience, giving rise to the Surrealist movement.

Surrealism was more than an art style; it was a philosophy, a way of thinking that embraced the irrational, the dreamlike, and the fantastical. Inspired by Freud's theories, Surrealists aimed to bypass the constraints of logic and reason, accessing deeper layers of the psyche where imagination could roam freely. The movement's manifesto, penned by André Breton in 1924, declared Surrealism to be a "pure psychic automatism" intended to express thought unfiltered by the conscious mind. This radical approach challenged traditional notions of art, reality, and creativity.

At the heart of Surrealism lay the concept of the dream. Freud's work, particularly *The Interpretation of Dreams* (1900), argued that dreams were a window into the unconscious, a space where repressed thoughts and emotions could manifest in symbolic form. Surrealists embraced this idea, using dreams as both inspiration and method. Their works often featured strange juxtapositions, impossible scenarios, and imagery that felt simultaneously familiar and alien, mirroring the logic, or illogic, of the unconscious mind.

One of the most iconic examples of Surrealist art is Salvador Dalí's *The Persistence of Memory* (1931), a painting that has become synonymous with the movement. In this work, Dalí depicted a barren landscape populated by melting clocks, a haunting blend of solidity and fluidity that seems to defy the laws of physics. The image evokes the malleability of time in dreams, where minutes can stretch into hours or vanish in an instant. The painting's unsettling atmosphere draws viewers into a world that feels both deeply personal and universally recognisable, a reflection of the shared human experience of dreaming.

René Magritte, another central figure in Surrealism, took a more conceptual approach. In works like *The Treachery of Images* (1929), Magritte challenged the relationship between objects and their representations. The painting features a simple image of a pipe accompanied by the text "Ceci n'est pas une pipe" ("This is not a pipe"). The statement, both true and perplexing, forces viewers to confront the gap between the object itself and its depiction. Magritte's work, like much of Surrealism, plays with the boundaries of perception and reality, encouraging viewers to question their assumptions.

The appeal of Surrealism lies in its ability to engage both the conscious and unconscious mind. At a cognitive level, the brain's recursive processes are activated as it tries to reconcile the disparate elements of a Surrealist work. A melting clock, a floating apple, or a headless figure demands interpretation, prompting the mind to loop through layers of meaning and symbolism. This recursive engagement mirrors the process of dreaming, where fragmented images and sensations are woven into narratives that are only partially comprehensible.

Physiologically, Surrealism evokes a complex interplay between the sympathetic and parasympathetic branches of the autonomic nervous system. The uncanny quality of Surrealist art, the way it combines the familiar and the strange, often triggers a mild sympathetic response. Viewers might feel a sense of unease or heightened alertness, a reaction rooted in the brain's instinct to detect and respond to anomalies in the environment. At the same time, the dreamlike aesthetics of Surrealism engage the parasympathetic system, fostering a sense of introspection and calm. This oscillation between arousal and relaxation mirrors the rhythm of REM sleep, where vivid dreams are accompanied by deep physical rest.

The cultural context of Surrealism also played a significant role in its development and resonance. Emerging in the aftermath of World War I, the movement reflected a world disillusioned with rationality and order, ideals that had failed to prevent the horrors of the war. Surrealism offered an alternative, celebrating the irrational and the imaginative as sources of truth and freedom. This ethos resonated with a generation seeking to rebuild their sense of identity and meaning in the face of global trauma.

Surrealism's influence extended far beyond the visual arts, shaping literature, film, and even psychology itself. Writers like Franz Kafka and James Joyce experimented with narrative structures that mimicked the flow of unconscious thought, while filmmakers like Luis Buñuel used cinema to create surreal, disorienting experiences. Buñuel's *Un Chien Andalou* (1929), co-created with Dalí, remains one of the most iconic examples of Surrealist cinema, its fragmented, dreamlike sequences challenging viewers to make sense of its deliberately ambiguous narrative.

In psychology, Freud's theories were both embraced and critiqued by later thinkers, but the idea of the unconscious as a source of creativity endured. Surrealism, in turn, influenced therapeutic approaches that sought to unlock the unconscious through techniques like free association and dream analysis. The recursive loops of thought encouraged by Surrealist art became tools for self-discovery, allowing individuals to explore the hidden layers of their psyche.

The enduring legacy of Surrealism lies in its ability to connect the rational and the irrational, the conscious and the unconscious. By embracing the logic of dreams and the mysteries of the mind,

Surrealism expanded the boundaries of what art could be, creating a space where imagination could flourish unencumbered by the constraints of reality. In a world increasingly dominated by technology and rationalism, the movement's emphasis on the fantastical and the personal remains as relevant as ever.

Through its strange, beautiful, and often unsettling imagery, Surrealism invites us to explore the depths of our own minds, to embrace the contradictions and complexities that define human experience. Like a dream, it defies easy interpretation, leaving us with fragments to ponder, patterns to uncover, and questions to carry with us long after we wake.

Chapter 7: Abstract Expressionism and the Atomic Bomb

The mid-twentieth century was an era of unprecedented upheaval, marked by the trauma of two world wars and the advent of a terrifying new force: the atomic bomb. The detonation of nuclear weapons over Hiroshima and Nagasaki in 1945 not only ended World War II but also signalled the dawn of an age in which humanity possessed the power to annihilate itself. This existential dread permeated global consciousness, altering the way people thought about progress, technology, and the fragility of human existence.

Against this backdrop, a group of artists in the United States began to experiment with new forms of expression that eschewed representation in favour of raw emotion and spontaneity. Known as Abstract Expressionism, this movement sought to capture the chaos and uncertainty of the modern age, offering a visceral response to the psychological landscape of the post-war world. Central to Abstract Expressionism was the idea that art could serve as an outlet for the subconscious, a space where unfiltered emotion could manifest in its purest form.

One of the defining characteristics of Abstract Expressionism is its embrace of scale and gesture. Paintings by figures like Jackson Pollock, Willem de Kooning, and Mark Rothko are often monumental in size, enveloping the viewer in a field of colour, texture, and motion. Pollock's drip paintings, for example, transform the canvas into an arena of action, where paint is flung and poured in dynamic, seemingly chaotic patterns. These works are not about representing external reality; they are about evoking an internal state, a raw and immediate experience that defies conventional interpretation.

The connection between Abstract Expressionism and the atomic age lies in their shared engagement with existential uncertainty. The bomb introduced a level of unpredictability and vulnerability that had no precedent in human history. Its power was invisible yet omnipresent, a force that could obliterate entire cities in an instant. Abstract Expressionism mirrors this tension, its fractured forms and chaotic lines reflecting a world where stability and permanence seemed illusory.

At a cognitive level, Abstract Expressionism engages the brain's recursive processes by presenting patterns that are both complex and incomplete. Pollock's drip paintings, for instance, consist of interwoven lines that suggest movement and depth but resist resolution. The viewer's brain is drawn into a loop of interpretation, seeking coherence in the apparent chaos. This recursive engagement mirrors the psychological grappling that characterised the atomic age, as people tried to make sense of a world where the old certainties no longer applied.

The autonomic nervous system also plays a crucial role in shaping the viewer's experience of Abstract Expressionism. The initial encounter with these works often triggers a sympathetic response, as the chaotic forms and intense colours stimulate arousal and alertness. Yet, as the viewer spends more time with the painting, the parasympathetic system begins to assert itself, allowing for reflection and introspection. This oscillation between arousal and calm creates a sense of dynamic engagement, mirroring the emotional rhythms of a world grappling with existential threats.

Mark Rothko's work represents a different, yet complementary, aspect of Abstract Expressionism. Unlike Pollock's frenetic energy, Rothko's paintings are characterised by large, softly defined fields of colour that seem to float and blend into one another. These works evoke a sense of stillness and introspection, inviting viewers to immerse themselves in the emotional resonance of the colours.

Rothko's canvases often elicit a profound sense of connection or contemplation, engaging the parasympathetic system to foster a state of calm reflection.

The cultural context of Abstract Expressionism was also deeply intertwined with the geopolitical realities of the Cold War. As the United States emerged as a global superpower, Abstract Expressionism became a symbol of American freedom and innovation. The movement's emphasis on individual expression and spontaneity was often contrasted with the rigidity and conformity associated with Soviet art, making it a cultural weapon in the ideological battles of the era. This political dimension, while often overlooked, underscores the extent to which art and power are interwoven.

Yet the legacy of Abstract Expressionism is far more than a reflection of its time. The movement's embrace of emotion, spontaneity, and ambiguity has had a lasting impact on the way we think about creativity and the role of the artist. By rejecting traditional forms and embracing the unpredictable, Abstract Expressionism challenged the notion that art must be orderly or representational. Instead, it opened up new possibilities for artistic expression, allowing artists to explore the depths of their emotions and the complexities of the human experience.

Abstract Expressionism's relevance extends beyond the canvas. Its emphasis on process over product has influenced fields as diverse as literature, music, and design. In literature, stream-of-consciousness techniques echo the movement's spontaneous gestures, while in music, improvisational jazz mirrors its dynamic interplay of structure and freedom. Even in contemporary digital art, the principles of Abstract Expressionism can be seen in generative designs that prioritise process and emergence over fixed outcomes.

The connection between Abstract Expressionism and the atomic bomb reminds us of art's ability to grapple with the most profound questions of human existence. In the face of destruction, chaos, and uncertainty, these artists chose to create, transforming their fear and frustration into works that continue to resonate with audiences today. Their paintings are not answers; they are questions, invitations to engage with the emotions and uncertainties that define what it means to be human.

Through its bold gestures and raw emotion, Abstract Expressionism captures the essence of an era defined by both terror and possibility. It reminds us that even in the most uncertain times, creativity can offer a path forward, a way to confront the unknown and find meaning in the act of expression itself.

Chapter 8: Pop Art and Mass Media

As the world transitioned from the upheavals of war and existential dread into the post-war boom of the mid-twentieth century, a new cultural phenomenon emerged: mass media. The proliferation of television, advertising, and consumer goods reshaped daily life, creating a reality where people were constantly surrounded by images and products that defined modern consumer culture. This flood of repetitive, highly curated visuals marked a departure from the naturalistic rhythms of earlier eras and introduced a hyper-mediated world. It was in this context that Pop Art emerged, a movement that reflected, critiqued, and celebrated the aesthetics of consumerism and mass media.

Pop Art was born in the 1950s and 1960s, primarily in the United States and the United Kingdom. Artists like Andy Warhol, Roy Lichtenstein, and Claes Oldenburg used the imagery of popular culture, soup cans, comic strips, advertisements, to create works that blurred the boundaries between high art and everyday life. The movement's name itself was a nod to its focus on the "popular," an embrace of the imagery and language of mass production that defined the age.

At the heart of Pop Art was a fascination with repetition and replication. Andy Warhol's iconic works, such as his *Campbell's Soup Cans* series and his silkscreen portraits of Marilyn Monroe, exemplify this aesthetic. By presenting rows of identical soup cans or repeated images of a celebrity's face, Warhol mimicked the visual language of advertising and mass production. Yet, these works were more than mere reproductions. They invited viewers to consider the cultural significance of these objects and images, to reflect on the ways in which consumer goods and media icons had come to dominate modern life.

The influence of mass media on Pop Art cannot be overstated. By the 1960s, television had become a ubiquitous presence in homes, shaping how people saw the world and themselves. Advertisements promised happiness, beauty, and fulfilment, turning products into symbols of aspiration. Pop Art mirrored this phenomenon, using the bold colours, clean lines, and graphic compositions of advertising to create works that were instantly recognisable. Yet, beneath the surface, the movement often critiqued the very culture it depicted, exposing the artificiality and emptiness that lay beneath the glossy exterior of consumerism.

Roy Lichtenstein's comic-inspired paintings highlight this tension between celebration and critique. Works like *Whaam!* and *Drowning Girl* replicate the aesthetic of comic book panels, complete with speech bubbles and exaggerated emotional expressions. Yet, by isolating these images and presenting them on a monumental scale, Lichtenstein transformed them into something both familiar and strange. The viewer is forced to confront the simplicity and melodrama of these narratives, reflecting on the ways in which mass media shapes emotional and cultural experiences.

Pop Art's engagement with mass production extended beyond its subject matter to its methods. Warhol's use of silkscreen printing allowed him to create multiple versions of the same image, mirroring the reproducibility of consumer goods. This technique challenged traditional notions of artistic authenticity, raising questions about originality and authorship. If a Warhol print of *Marilyn Monroe* was created in a factory-like studio and existed in multiple copies, was it still "art"? For Warhol, the answer was an emphatic yes. By embracing the tools and techniques of mass production, he argued, art could better reflect the realities of the modern world.

At a cognitive level, Pop Art engages the brain's recursive processes by playing with familiarity and novelty. The repetition of recognisable images draws on existing patterns in the viewer's memory, creating an immediate sense of connection. Yet, the context and scale of these images introduce an element of surprise, forcing the brain to reinterpret what it sees. This interplay between the familiar and the unexpected mirrors the recursive loops of thought that define human cognition, making Pop Art both accessible and thought-provoking.

Physiologically, Pop Art engages the autonomic nervous system in a unique way. The bold colours and graphic designs stimulate the sympathetic system, creating a sense of energy and excitement. At the same time, the repetitive nature of the imagery can have a calming effect, engaging the parasympathetic system and fostering a sense of rhythm and order. This balance between arousal and relaxation is key to Pop Art's appeal, making it both stimulating and reassuring.

The cultural context of Pop Art was inseparable from the economic prosperity of the post-war era. In the United States, the 1950s and 1960s were marked by a consumer boom, fuelled by rising incomes and the proliferation of suburban living. Shopping malls, television commercials, and brand loyalty became defining features of the American lifestyle. Pop Art reflected this reality, transforming the symbols of consumer culture into objects of artistic inquiry.

Yet, Pop Art was not limited to celebration. Many works subtly critiqued the culture they depicted. Warhol's *Death and Disaster* series, for example, used the same silkscreen techniques he employed for his celebrity portraits to reproduce images of car crashes and electric chairs. By juxtaposing the language of consumerism with themes of mortality and violence, Warhol exposed the darker undercurrents of a culture obsessed with surface appearances.

Pop Art also challenged traditional hierarchies of taste and value. By elevating everyday objects and commercial imagery to the status of fine art, the movement questioned what it meant to create and appreciate art in the modern age. Was a painting of a soup can less valuable than a Renaissance portrait? Could a comic strip panel be as significant as a classical sculpture? These questions, raised by Pop Art, continue to resonate in contemporary discussions about art and culture.

The legacy of Pop Art extends far beyond the 1960s. Its influence can be seen in everything from graphic design to fashion, from advertising to digital media. The movement's embrace of consumer culture laid the groundwork for postmodern art, which continues to explore the intersections of commerce, identity, and creativity. In a world increasingly defined by screens and social media, Pop Art's exploration of repetition, replication, and visual language feels more relevant than ever.

Ultimately, Pop Art reflects a world where the lines between art and life, originality and reproduction, have become blurred. It invites us to reconsider our relationship with the images and objects that surround us, to see the extraordinary in the ordinary and the complexity in the seemingly simple. Through its bold, playful, and often provocative works, Pop Art captures the spirit of an age defined by mass media, a spirit that continues to shape the way we see and create today.

Chapter 9: Minimalism and Industrial Design

As the twentieth century progressed, the relentless pace of industrialisation and the increasing complexity of modern life gave rise to a counter-movement in art and design: Minimalism. Rooted in the principles of simplicity, clarity, and functionality, Minimalism emerged as a response to the sensory and cultural overload of the post-war world. It sought to strip away excess, focusing instead on the essential elements of form and space. In doing so, Minimalism reflected not only a shift in aesthetic values but also a profound rethinking of how humans interacted with their environments.

Minimalism's roots can be traced back to earlier modernist movements, particularly the Bauhaus school of design, which emphasised the union of art, craftsmanship, and technology. However, it was in the 1960s and 1970s that Minimalism came into its own as a distinct movement. Artists like Donald Judd, Dan Flavin, and Agnes Martin rejected the emotive, gestural approaches of Abstract Expressionism, favouring clean lines, geometric forms, and repetition. Minimalist works often sought to eliminate the artist's hand entirely, creating pieces that appeared impersonal and objective.

In parallel, industrial design embraced similar principles, particularly in response to the demands of mass production and modern functionality. Designers like Dieter Rams, whose "less, but better" philosophy became iconic, created objects that prioritised usability and clarity over ornamentation. The emergence of Minimalism in both art and design reflected a broader cultural shift toward simplicity, efficiency, and the pursuit of harmony in a rapidly changing world.

At the heart of Minimalism lies an exploration of space, both the physical space occupied by objects and the conceptual space they inhabit. In a world increasingly cluttered with information, noise, and material goods, Minimalism offered a sense of clarity and stillness. The movement's focus on negative space, the emptiness surrounding an object, invited viewers and users to pause, to breathe, and to engage more deeply with their surroundings. This emphasis on space and simplicity resonated with a society grappling with the chaotic aftermath of industrialisation and technological expansion.

Minimalist art often engages the viewer's perception in subtle yet profound ways. Donald Judd's sculptures, for instance, consist of repeated geometric forms, stacks, cubes, and rectangles, arranged with precise intervals. These works are not intended to represent anything; instead, they exist as pure forms, inviting viewers to contemplate their structure and spatial relationships. Similarly, Dan Flavin's installations, composed of fluorescent light tubes, transform gallery spaces with their ethereal glow, creating environments that feel both industrial and transcendent.

The viewer's experience of Minimalism is deeply tied to the brain's recursive processes. By stripping away extraneous details, Minimalist works focus attention on fundamental elements, lines, shapes, colours, that the brain processes with clarity and precision. This simplicity allows for deeper recursive engagement, as the viewer reflects on the relationships between form and space, light and shadow, presence and absence. The recursive mind, freed from the need to interpret complex imagery, finds itself in a state of meditative exploration.

Physiologically, Minimalism engages the autonomic nervous system in a uniquely calming way. The clean lines and repetitive forms of

Minimalist art and design activate the parasympathetic system, promoting relaxation and focus. Unlike movements that rely on dramatic contrasts or emotional intensity, Minimalism creates an environment of balance and order. This sense of tranquillity makes it particularly appealing in a world often dominated by overstimulation and chaos.

The principles of Minimalism found a natural home in industrial design, where they were applied to objects ranging from furniture to electronics. Dieter Rams, a key figure in the movement, created designs for Braun that epitomised Minimalist aesthetics. His radios, clocks, and kitchen appliances were characterised by clean lines, functional simplicity, and an intuitive interface. Rams' influence can be seen in the work of later designers, most notably Jonathan Ive, whose designs for Apple brought Minimalism into the digital age.

Minimalism's emphasis on simplicity and functionality also extended to architecture. Figures like Ludwig Mies van der Rohe and Tadao Ando created buildings that celebrated the beauty of unadorned materials and open spaces. Mies van der Rohe's famous dictum, "less is more," encapsulated the ethos of the movement, which sought to create environments that were both serene and purposeful. Ando, working primarily in concrete, used light, shadow, and geometry to craft spaces that felt contemplative and timeless.

The cultural appeal of Minimalism lies in its ability to create a sense of order and clarity in a world that often feels overwhelming. By reducing objects and spaces to their essential elements, Minimalism offers a respite from the clutter of modern life. This aesthetic of simplicity resonates not only in physical spaces but also in digital environments, where Minimalist design principles guide the interfaces of smartphones, websites, and applications.

However, Minimalism is not without its critics. Some argue that its focus on simplicity and functionality can feel cold or impersonal, prioritising aesthetics over emotional connection. Others see it as a reflection of privilege, an aesthetic accessible only to those who can afford to choose "less." These critiques highlight the tension inherent in Minimalism, a movement that seeks to universalise beauty and functionality while operating within the constraints of specific cultural and economic contexts.

Despite these challenges, the legacy of Minimalism endures, influencing fields as diverse as fashion, technology, and environmental design. Its principles have been adapted to address contemporary concerns, from sustainability to mindfulness. In architecture, Minimalism has inspired the tiny house movement, which emphasises simplicity and efficiency as a response to overconsumption. In technology, it has shaped the clean, intuitive interfaces that define modern digital experiences.

Ultimately, Minimalism reflects a desire to find clarity amidst complexity, to create harmony in a world of competing demands. Its emphasis on the essential invites us to reconsider what we truly need and value, both in our surroundings and in ourselves. By stripping away the unnecessary, Minimalism reveals the beauty of the fundamental, the quiet elegance of a single line, the profound stillness of an empty space. In doing so, it offers not just an aesthetic, but a philosophy, a way of seeing and living that resonates across time and disciplines.

Chapter 10: Digital Art and the Internet

The late twentieth century ushered in a technological revolution that transformed nearly every aspect of human life. With the advent of computers, the internet, and later, digital media, the ways in which people created, consumed, and interacted with art changed in unprecedented ways. No longer confined to traditional mediums like canvas or film, art entered a realm of pixels, algorithms, and virtual spaces, redefining what it meant to create and experience. This transformation gave rise to digital art, a movement that both reflected and shaped the digital age.

Digital art emerged as computers became more accessible in the 1980s and 1990s, but its roots can be traced to earlier experiments in technology and creativity. Artists in the mid-twentieth century had already begun exploring the possibilities of electronic media, creating works that fused traditional art with emerging technologies. However, the exponential growth of computing power and the spread of the internet in the latter part of the century allowed digital art to flourish as a distinct form, characterised by its use of digital tools and platforms.

Unlike traditional art forms, digital art exists in a medium that is inherently fluid and dynamic. It can be interactive, generative, or immersive, inviting viewers to engage in ways that were previously unimaginable. A digital painting, for example, can change in real-time based on the viewer's movements or input, while an algorithmic artwork might continuously evolve, creating new forms and patterns long after its initial creation. These possibilities reflect the recursive nature of digital technology itself, which operates through loops, iterations, and feedback systems that mirror the processes of the human brain.

One of the defining features of digital art is its relationship with the internet. The internet not only serves as a medium for the creation and dissemination of digital works but also as a source of inspiration and material. Artists often draw on the vast archives of images, data, and code available online, remixing and reinterpreting them to create new works. This process mirrors the way the brain integrates and reconfigures sensory inputs, engaging recursive loops to generate meaning from a constant stream of information.

The interactive nature of digital art also transforms the role of the viewer. In traditional art, the viewer is often a passive observer, engaging with a static object or image. In digital art, however, the viewer often becomes a participant, influencing or even co-creating the work. For example, Rafael Lozano-Hemmer's interactive installations use sensors to respond to the presence and movements of viewers, creating a dynamic interplay between the artwork and its audience. This interactivity reflects the recursive engagement of the mind, as viewers not only interpret the work but also contribute to its evolution.

Physiologically, digital art engages the autonomic nervous system in complex and layered ways. The immersive environments created by virtual reality (VR) or augmented reality (AR) artworks often trigger sympathetic responses, heightening arousal and attention. At the same time, the meditative qualities of generative art or slow, interactive installations can engage the parasympathetic system, promoting relaxation and introspection. This dynamic interplay creates a uniquely multifaceted experience, appealing to both the sensory and cognitive aspects of the viewer's engagement.

One of the most significant contributions of digital art is its ability to explore themes that are uniquely tied to the digital age. Issues like data privacy, artificial intelligence, and the ethics of technology have become central to contemporary life, and digital artists have been at the forefront of addressing these questions. Works like Trevor Paglen's explorations of surveillance systems or Refik Anadol's data-driven visualisations highlight the ways in which technology shapes human experience, using the medium of digital art to critique and reflect on its own implications.

The internet has also democratised access to art in ways that were previously unimaginable. Digital platforms allow artists to share their work with a global audience, bypassing traditional gatekeepers like galleries and museums. Social media platforms, in particular, have become spaces where digital art thrives, creating communities of creators and viewers who engage with art in real-time. This shift has blurred the boundaries between professional and amateur, high art and popular culture, creating a vibrant and diverse ecosystem of creativity.

At the same time, the rise of digital art has raised questions about authorship, originality, and value. In a medium where works can be infinitely copied and reproduced, what does it mean for a piece of art to be "authentic"? These questions have gained new urgency with the advent of blockchain technology and non-fungible tokens (NFTs), which have introduced new ways of establishing ownership and provenance for digital works. While NFTs have been celebrated for empowering artists and creating new markets, they have also sparked debates about environmental impact and the commodification of digital creativity.

The legacy of digital art lies in its ability to push the boundaries of what art can be. By embracing the tools and technologies of the digital age, it has expanded the possibilities of creation and experience, allowing artists to explore new dimensions of space, time, and interaction. At the same time, digital art challenges viewers to reconsider their relationship with technology, prompting them to reflect on the ways in which it shapes their perceptions, emotions, and identities.

Ultimately, digital art is not just a reflection of the digital age; it is an integral part of it, shaping and being shaped by the technologies and cultures of the time. As algorithms become more sophisticated and virtual spaces more immersive, the boundaries between art and technology will continue to blur, creating new possibilities for creativity and connection. In this ever-evolving landscape, digital art stands as a testament to the power of human imagination, a reminder that even in the most technologically advanced age, the act of creation remains profoundly human.

Chapter 11: Why We Like What We Like

Human preferences are as unique as fingerprints, yet they follow discernible patterns that can be traced to the interplay of biology, culture, and individual experience. The question of why we like what we like, whether in art, music, design, or even daily objects, is deeply rooted in the workings of the brain, the autonomic nervous system, and the cultural frameworks we inhabit. Preferences are not random; they are the result of recursive processes in the mind, shaped by a dynamic interplay between familiarity, novelty, and emotional resonance.

At its core, the human brain is a pattern-seeking organ. It constantly scans the environment for recognisable forms, rhythms, and relationships, using predictive coding to anticipate what comes next. This process is essential for survival, allowing us to navigate the world efficiently and respond to changes. In the realm of aesthetics, this same mechanism drives our enjoyment of patterns that align with or slightly disrupt our expectations. A symphony that follows a familiar structure but introduces surprising variations, or a painting that balances recognisable forms with abstract elements, activates the brain's reward systems, creating pleasure.

Familiarity plays a key role in shaping preferences. The more often we are exposed to a certain style, form, or idea, the more likely we are to find it appealing, a phenomenon known as the mere-exposure effect. This principle explains why certain genres of music or art become more enjoyable with repeated listening or viewing. Familiarity provides a sense of comfort and security, engaging the parasympathetic nervous system to create a calming effect. It also enhances the brain's ability to process stimuli efficiently, reducing cognitive load and allowing us to focus on subtler details.

However, familiarity alone is not enough to sustain interest. Novelty, the element of surprise or deviation from expectation, is equally important. Art and experiences that introduce unexpected elements engage the sympathetic nervous system, triggering arousal and curiosity. This tension between familiarity and novelty is at the heart of many artistic movements. Impressionism, for example, balanced the recognisable forms of landscapes and human figures with an innovative approach to light, colour, and brushwork, creating works that were both accessible and groundbreaking.

The recursive mind plays a central role in balancing these elements. When we encounter something new, our brain mirrors and refines the sensory input, comparing it to stored patterns and integrating it into our mental framework. This process is iterative, allowing us to revisit and reinterpret the experience over time. A novel piece of music or art might initially seem strange or dissonant, but with repeated exposure, the brain's recursive loops find harmony within the novelty, transforming it into something we enjoy.

Emotional resonance is another critical factor in determining what we like. The autonomic nervous system shapes our visceral responses to stimuli, creating feelings of excitement, calm, or even discomfort. Colours, shapes, and sounds that evoke positive emotions are more likely to be preferred, as they align with the brain's reward circuits. For example, warm colours like red and yellow often evoke feelings of energy and joy, while cool colours like blue and green promote relaxation. These responses are not universal, however; they are influenced by personal experiences and cultural associations. A colour that feels soothing in one culture may carry negative connotations in another.

The role of memory in shaping preferences cannot be overstated. Experiences from childhood, significant life events, and emotional milestones all leave imprints on the brain, creating associations that influence our likes and dislikes. A song heard during a joyful moment may become a lifelong favourite, while a smell associated with a negative memory might evoke discomfort. These associations are reinforced through recursive reflection, as the brain revisits and reinterprets past experiences in light of new ones.

Cultural frameworks also play a pivotal role in shaping preferences. The values, symbols, and narratives of a society influence what is considered beautiful, meaningful, or desirable. In the Renaissance, the ideal of symmetry and proportion reflected a cultural emphasis on harmony and rationality. In the modern era, the fragmented perspectives of Cubism resonated with a world grappling with the complexities of time and space. Our individual preferences are shaped by these larger cultural currents, even as we interpret them through the lens of our personal experiences.

Social context further amplifies the influence of culture. People often gravitate toward what others around them enjoy, a phenomenon driven by the human desire for connection and belonging. This dynamic can create trends and fads, where certain styles or genres become widely popular before fading into obscurity. The rise of Pop Art, for example, was not only a reflection of consumer culture but also a response to the collective tastes of a media-saturated society. The recursive loops of social influence reinforce these preferences, creating feedback systems that shape cultural norms.

However, preferences are not static; they evolve over time. Exposure to new stimuli, changing life circumstances, and shifts in cultural context all contribute to the fluid nature of what we like and dislike. The brain's plasticity, the ability to adapt and form new connections, allows us to expand our preferences, embracing forms and ideas that once felt alien. This adaptability is particularly evident in art, where movements that were initially controversial often become celebrated as cultural milestones. Impressionism, once dismissed as amateurish, is now revered as a cornerstone of modern art.

Understanding why we like what we like requires recognising the interplay between these various factors. It is not merely a matter of individual taste but a complex interaction of biology, psychology, and culture. The recursive mind integrates sensory input, emotional responses, and cultural frameworks, creating a dynamic web of preferences that evolves throughout our lives. By examining this process, we gain insight not only into our own likes and dislikes but also into the shared human experience of finding meaning and beauty in the world around us.

In the chapters ahead, we will explore how these principles extend beyond art to other domains of life, music, design, food, and even social interactions. By delving deeper into the factors that shape our preferences, we can begin to understand the intricate connections between mind, body, and culture, revealing the profound ways in which we engage with and interpret the world.

Chapter 12: Why We Dislike What We Dislike

Just as our preferences are shaped by the interplay of cognitive processes, emotional resonance, and cultural frameworks, so too are our aversions. Disliking something is often seen as the inverse of liking, but it is a far more nuanced phenomenon. Where enjoyment arises from a balance of familiarity, novelty, and emotional satisfaction, dislike often stems from an imbalance, whether in the form of cognitive overload, emotional dissonance, or cultural misalignment. Understanding why we dislike certain things reveals not only the boundaries of our preferences but also the ways in which these boundaries can shift and evolve.

At its core, dislike begins in the brain, where sensory inputs are processed and evaluated. The brain's predictive coding system seeks to match incoming stimuli with existing patterns, generating predictions about what to expect. When these predictions are dramatically violated, whether through excessive complexity, incongruity, or unpleasant associations, the result can be discomfort or even aversion. For example, a discordant piece of music might overwhelm the brain's ability to find harmony, triggering a negative response. Similarly, a chaotic painting might feel unsettling because it challenges the brain's need for order and coherence.

This cognitive discomfort is often accompanied by a physiological response, governed by the autonomic nervous system. Dislike typically activates the sympathetic nervous system, the branch responsible for the body's fight-or-flight response. When confronted with stimuli that feel threatening, disorienting, or otherwise unpleasant, the sympathetic system prepares the body for action, increasing heart rate and alertness. This response is not always extreme; it can manifest as a subtle sense of unease or irritation. In contrast, stimuli that engage the parasympathetic system, promoting relaxation and calm, are less likely to elicit dislike.

One of the most common sources of aversion is **cognitive overload**, which occurs when the brain is unable to process stimuli effectively. This can happen when a work of art, a piece of music, or even a conversation is too complex, chaotic, or unfamiliar. Abstract Expressionism, for instance, can feel overwhelming to viewers who are unaccustomed to its raw, emotive gestures and lack of representational structure. The brain struggles to find patterns or meaning, leading to frustration or disengagement. Similarly, highly experimental music with dissonant tones and irregular rhythms may feel jarring to those whose auditory preferences lean toward harmony and predictability.

The opposite of cognitive overload, **monotony**, can also lead to dislike. When stimuli are too simple or repetitive, they fail to engage the brain's predictive coding system, creating boredom. Minimalist art and design, while celebrated by many for their elegance and clarity, can feel dull or uninspiring to those who crave complexity and variety. This aversion arises from the brain's need for stimulation and novelty, which is unfulfilled by overly simplistic or unchanging patterns.

Beyond cognitive factors, **emotional dissonance** plays a significant role in shaping aversions. The autonomic nervous system reacts strongly to stimuli that conflict with an individual's emotional state or expectations. For example, a horror film might feel thrilling to someone seeking excitement but deeply unsettling to someone in search of comfort. Similarly, art that evokes painful or negative emotions, such as Francis Bacon's grotesque and visceral paintings, can provoke aversion in viewers who are unprepared to confront such imagery.

Cultural and personal associations further amplify emotional dissonance. A style of music or a type of food that is celebrated in one culture might be met with aversion in another, simply because it does not align with the listener's or eater's cultural framework. These aversions are not fixed; they are shaped by experience and exposure. For instance, a Western listener who initially finds traditional Indian ragas unfamiliar and overwhelming might come to appreciate their complexity and beauty with repeated exposure and cultural understanding.

Personal memories and experiences also influence dislike. Negative associations formed in childhood or during significant life events can leave lasting imprints on the brain, shaping aversions that persist into adulthood. A person who was forced to eat a particular food as a child might develop a lifelong distaste for it, even if they recognise its quality or nutritional value. Similarly, a traumatic experience linked to a specific place, sound, or smell can create a strong aversion to anything that evokes that memory. These emotional imprints are reinforced by the brain's recursive processes, which revisit and reframe past experiences, making aversions deeply personal and often resistant to change.

Dislike is also influenced by **social and cultural context**. Just as people gravitate toward what is popular or celebrated within their community, they often reject what is perceived as outside the norm. This dynamic can create biases against unfamiliar styles, genres, or ideas, particularly those associated with other cultures or subcultures. The initial backlash against Impressionism, for instance, reflected a cultural preference for realism and historical themes. Similarly, avant-garde movements like Dada and Cubism were initially met with scepticism or hostility because they defied the conventions of their time.

However, aversions are not static; they can evolve over time. The same mechanisms that shape preferences, exposure, reflection, and cultural adaptation, can transform dislikes into likes. This phenomenon, known as "acquired taste," occurs when repeated exposure to a stimulus allows the brain to integrate it into its predictive coding system. For example, a person who initially dislikes bitter foods like coffee or dark chocolate may come to enjoy them as they develop an appreciation for their complexity. Similarly, exposure to a challenging art form, such as Surrealism or jazz, can lead to greater understanding and enjoyment over time.

The process of overcoming aversion often involves a shift in context or perspective. A viewer who initially finds abstract art perplexing might come to appreciate it after learning about the artist's intent or the cultural context in which it was created. Similarly, a piece of music that feels dissonant on first listen might become enjoyable after the listener gains familiarity with its structure and themes. These shifts are facilitated by the brain's plasticity, which allows for the formation of new neural connections and the integration of novel patterns.

Ultimately, dislike is not merely a rejection of something unfamiliar or unpleasant; it is a reflection of the dynamic interplay between cognition, emotion, and culture. By examining the sources of our aversions, we can gain a deeper understanding of our preferences and expand our capacity for appreciation. Dislike, in this sense, is not a limitation but an opportunity, a starting point for growth and exploration.

In the chapters ahead, we will explore how these principles of liking and disliking extend to broader domains, from food and fashion to social interactions and personal identity. By understanding the mechanisms that shape our aversions, we can learn to challenge our assumptions, expand our horizons, and engage more deeply with the world around us.

Chapter 13: The Role of Memory and Emotion

At the heart of what we like and dislike lies a complex web of memory and emotion. Every preference we hold, whether for a particular song, a type of cuisine, or a style of art, is shaped by past experiences. Memory serves as the repository of these experiences, while emotion imbues them with meaning, forging connections that can influence our responses for years, or even a lifetime. Together, memory and emotion create the rich, subjective landscape of our preferences.

The brain is a profoundly associative organ. When we encounter something, a melody, a scent, an image, it doesn't exist in isolation. Instead, the brain links it to past experiences stored in the hippocampus, the region of the brain responsible for forming and retrieving memories. These memories are not neutral; they are coloured by the emotions we felt at the time of the original experience, a process mediated by the amygdala. This pairing of memory and emotion creates a kind of shorthand for preference. A song associated with a joyful moment might evoke happiness whenever we hear it, while a smell linked to an unpleasant memory might trigger discomfort.

These emotional imprints often develop in childhood, a time when the brain is particularly plastic and sensitive to external influences. The foods we ate, the music we heard, the art we were exposed to, all of these early experiences shape the neural pathways that guide our preferences as adults. A person who grew up listening to classical music, for instance, might find comfort in its familiar structures, while someone who was exposed to jazz from a young age might have a greater tolerance for improvisation and dissonance.

The recursive nature of the brain plays a critical role in this process. Each time we revisit a memory, the brain not only retrieves it but also reshapes it, integrating new information and associations. This is why our preferences can evolve over time. A song that once reminded us of a heartbreak might take on new meaning as we create positive memories around it, while an artwork that initially felt perplexing might become enjoyable as we learn more about its context and significance.

Emotion serves as the compass that guides our preferences, steering us toward experiences that align with our current state of mind or desired emotional outcomes. When we're feeling joyful, we might gravitate toward upbeat music, bright colours, or lively conversations that amplify that feeling. Conversely, when we're seeking solace, we might prefer slower, quieter stimuli that evoke calm and introspection. This emotional alignment engages the parasympathetic nervous system, promoting relaxation and reinforcing positive associations.

However, emotion doesn't just influence our likes; it also plays a significant role in shaping our dislikes. Negative experiences can leave powerful imprints, creating aversions that persist long after the original event. A person who had a traumatic encounter with a dog as a child might develop a lifelong fear of dogs, even if they rarely encounter them in adulthood. Similarly, a piece of music that played during a distressing moment might evoke unease or sadness, regardless of its inherent qualities.

The emotional intensity of an experience often determines the strength of the memory and its associated preference. Highly charged moments, whether joyful, sorrowful, or terrifying, are more likely to be remembered vividly, thanks to the brain's release of stress hormones like cortisol and adrenaline. These hormones heighten the amygdala's activity, encoding the experience more deeply. This is why people often have strong emotional connections to the music, films, or books they encountered during formative periods like adolescence, when emotions tend to run high.

Cultural narratives further shape the interplay between memory and emotion. Society provides shared frameworks that influence how we interpret and store experiences. For instance, a particular piece of classical music might evoke grandeur and sophistication because of its cultural associations, while a punk rock anthem might feel rebellious and energising. These narratives are reinforced by repetition, creating collective memories that influence individual preferences.

The power of memory and emotion to shape preferences is particularly evident in the realm of nostalgia. Nostalgia is a deeply emotional response, triggered by sensory cues that transport us back to a time or place associated with happiness or comfort. The scent of a favourite childhood meal, the opening notes of a beloved song, or the style of a retro fashion trend can evoke a profound sense of connection to the past. Nostalgia not only reinforces existing preferences but can also reshape them, making us more receptive to stimuli we might have otherwise overlooked.

At the same time, the brain's plasticity allows for the creation of new emotional associations, even later in life. A painting that initially seemed abstract and unapproachable might become a favourite after it's linked to a meaningful experience, such as a visit to a museum with a loved one. This ability to create new connections is one of the reasons our preferences can expand and evolve, even as they remain grounded in our past.

Memory and emotion also play a critical role in the social dimensions of preference. Shared experiences create collective memories that strengthen bonds between individuals and groups. A family tradition of listening to certain songs during holidays, for example, might create lasting emotional connections to those songs, reinforcing their significance. Similarly, cultural celebrations, like attending a concert or watching a popular film with friends, create shared emotional experiences that shape collective preferences.

Understanding the role of memory and emotion in shaping preferences allows us to appreciate the deeply personal and yet universal nature of what we like and dislike. Our preferences are not static; they are dynamic, evolving with each new experience and reinterpretation of the past. By exploring the memories and emotions that underlie our likes and dislikes, we can gain insight into ourselves and our connections to others.

In the chapters ahead, we will delve into the broader implications of these findings, exploring how preferences extend beyond art and aesthetics to influence our choices in food, fashion, relationships, and more. By examining the interplay between memory, emotion, and culture, we can begin to uncover the deeper patterns that define our engagement with the world.

Chapter 14: From Aversion to Appreciation

The journey from aversion to appreciation is one of the most fascinating aspects of human preference. What begins as a strong dislike can, over time, evolve into profound enjoyment or even love. This transformation, often referred to as acquiring a taste, reveals the brain's remarkable capacity for adaptation and learning. It highlights the interplay of exposure, context, and reflection in reshaping our perceptions, challenging us to embrace new experiences and expand our horizons.

At first glance, aversions seem fixed and insurmountable. The sharp bitterness of coffee, the dissonant tones of avant-garde music, or the abstraction of certain art styles can provoke immediate rejection. These initial responses are often rooted in cognitive overload or emotional dissonance. The unfamiliarity or intensity of a stimulus overwhelms the brain's ability to integrate it into existing patterns, triggering discomfort or disengagement. However, this aversion is rarely permanent. Through repeated exposure and shifts in context, the brain can reprocess and reinterpret stimuli, gradually transforming aversion into appreciation.

One of the primary mechanisms behind this transformation is the **mere-exposure effect**, the phenomenon whereby repeated encounters with a stimulus increase its appeal. Each exposure allows the brain's predictive coding system to become more familiar with the stimulus, reducing cognitive load and making the experience more comfortable. For instance, a person who initially finds jazz chaotic and unpredictable might, after repeated listening, begin to recognise its structure and rhythm, finding pleasure in its complexity. Similarly, a bitter food like dark chocolate may become enjoyable as the palate adjusts to its nuances.

Context also plays a critical role in overcoming aversion. The environment in which we encounter a stimulus can significantly influence how we perceive it. A painting that feels inaccessible in isolation might take on new meaning when seen in a museum, surrounded by works from the same movement or artist. Similarly, a challenging piece of music might become more enjoyable when heard in a live performance, where the energy of the musicians and audience creates a shared emotional experience. Context provides additional layers of information and meaning, helping the brain integrate the unfamiliar into a broader framework.

Social and cultural factors further shape the journey from aversion to appreciation. Preferences are not formed in a vacuum; they are influenced by the values and norms of the communities we inhabit. Exposure to diverse perspectives can challenge our assumptions and encourage us to reconsider our dislikes. For instance, a person who dislikes sushi might develop a taste for it after sharing a meal with friends who appreciate its flavours and traditions. This social reinforcement creates positive associations, strengthening the connection between the stimulus and enjoyment.

The recursive nature of the brain is central to this process of transformation. Each time we revisit a stimulus, whether it's a painting, a song, or a dish, the brain re-evaluates it in light of new information and experiences. This iterative process allows for the gradual refinement of perception, as the brain integrates the unfamiliar into existing patterns. Over time, what once felt alien or overwhelming can become familiar and even comforting. A person who initially struggles to appreciate abstract art, for example, might, through repeated exposure and reflection, come to find joy in its ambiguity and open-endedness.

Emotion also plays a pivotal role in shifting preferences. Positive emotional experiences associated with a previously disliked stimulus can help reframe it in a more favourable light. For example, a song that felt grating on first listen might become a favourite after it plays during a joyful moment, such as a celebration or reunion. Similarly, a food that was once unappealing might take on new significance after being prepared by a loved one. These emotional associations, reinforced by memory, create new pathways in the brain that shape future responses.

The transformation from aversion to appreciation is not limited to personal preferences; it is a recurring pattern in the history of art and culture. Many artistic movements that were initially met with resistance, Impressionism, Cubism, and Surrealism, to name a few, eventually became celebrated as groundbreaking innovations. This shift often occurs as society becomes more familiar with the movement's principles and context, allowing it to integrate the once-alien into the collective cultural framework.

Impressionism, for instance, was ridiculed by critics in its early days, dismissed as unfinished and amateurish. Yet, over time, audiences came to appreciate its emphasis on light, colour, and fleeting moments, recognising the movement's radical departure from traditional realism as a profound artistic achievement. This transformation mirrors the individual journey from aversion to appreciation, as exposure and understanding replace initial resistance with admiration.

Similarly, foods and flavours that are now widely beloved often began as acquired tastes. Spicy foods, for example, can be overwhelming to those unaccustomed to their heat, but with repeated exposure, the brain learns to associate the sensation of spice with pleasure rather than discomfort. Fermented foods, with their bold and sometimes pungent flavours, follow a similar trajectory. The process of acquiring a taste for such foods reflects the brain's ability to adapt and form new associations, expanding the boundaries of enjoyment.

Overcoming aversion is not merely a matter of endurance or repetition; it requires an openness to new experiences and a willingness to challenge preconceived notions. This openness, often fostered by curiosity and a sense of adventure, creates the conditions for growth and transformation. It allows us to move beyond the limitations of our initial reactions, embracing the unfamiliar and finding beauty in the unexpected.

The ability to transform aversion into appreciation is a testament to the brain's plasticity and the dynamic nature of human preference. It highlights the importance of exposure, context, and reflection in shaping our likes and dislikes, reminding us that preferences are not static but constantly evolving. By embracing this process, we can expand our horizons, deepening our engagement with the world and enriching our lives.

In the chapters ahead, we will explore how this capacity for transformation extends beyond individual preferences to influence broader cultural trends and societal values. By examining the ways in which preferences evolve over time, we can gain a deeper understanding of the forces that shape our collective tastes and the potential for growth and change within ourselves and our communities.

Chapter 15: The Next Wave of Creativity

As we stand on the cusp of an increasingly interconnected and technologically driven future, the next wave of creativity promises to redefine the boundaries of human expression. The tools and ideas that shape this new era, artificial intelligence, virtual reality, genetic engineering, and more, are as transformative as the inventions that inspired past artistic movements. Just as trains influenced Impressionism and mass media gave rise to Pop Art, these emerging technologies are poised to revolutionise not only how we create but also how we think about art, culture, and identity.

The impact of artificial intelligence (AI) on creativity is already becoming apparent. AI systems, such as generative adversarial networks (GANs) and natural language processing models, are capable of producing music, paintings, and even written works that rival those created by humans. Artists are increasingly collaborating with AI, using these tools to generate ideas, explore new forms, and push the boundaries of what is possible. This partnership between human and machine echoes the recursive processes of the brain, where iterative loops of reflection and refinement lead to innovation.

AI-generated art challenges traditional notions of authorship and originality. If a machine can create a painting or compose a symphony, who is the artist? Is it the machine, the programmer, or the person who selects and curates the output? These questions are not merely theoretical; they strike at the heart of what it means to create. For some, AI represents a threat to the uniqueness of human creativity. For others, it is a tool that expands the possibilities of artistic expression, enabling us to explore new dimensions of thought and imagination.

Virtual reality (VR) and augmented reality (AR) are also transforming the creative landscape. These immersive technologies allow artists to create environments that viewers can enter and interact with, blurring the lines between the real and the virtual. A VR artwork is not just something to be seen; it is an experience to be inhabited, engaging the senses and emotions in ways that traditional mediums cannot. This shift from passive observation to active participation mirrors the evolution of art itself, from static representations to dynamic, interactive forms.

The immersive nature of VR and AR also offers new possibilities for storytelling. In a virtual space, narratives can unfold in multiple dimensions, allowing viewers to explore different perspectives and paths. This non-linear approach to storytelling reflects the recursive nature of thought, where ideas loop back on themselves, creating layers of meaning. It also challenges traditional concepts of audience and author, as the viewer becomes an active participant in shaping the story.

Another frontier of creativity lies in the realm of genetic engineering and biotechnology. Advances in these fields are enabling artists to work with living materials, creating bio-art that blurs the boundaries between science and aesthetics. Artists like Eduardo Kac have used genetic modification to create living works, such as a fluorescent green rabbit named *Alba*. These projects raise profound questions about the ethics of manipulating life, as well as the role of art in exploring and challenging the boundaries of science.

The integration of biology into art also invites us to reconsider our relationship with nature. In an era of climate change and environmental degradation, bio-art offers a way to reflect on humanity's impact on the planet and explore new possibilities for coexistence. Living sculptures, sustainable materials, and biomimetic designs are just some of the ways artists are using creativity to address ecological concerns and envision a more harmonious future.

The role of the internet in shaping the next wave of creativity cannot be overstated. Online platforms have democratized access to art and culture, allowing creators to reach global audiences and collaborate across borders. At the same time, the internet has given rise to new forms of expression, from memes and digital installations to NFTs and virtual galleries. These digital-native art forms reflect the language and logic of the internet itself: fast, interconnected, and constantly evolving.

Non-fungible tokens (NFTs) represent one of the most controversial developments in the digital art world. By using blockchain technology to establish ownership and provenance, NFTs have created a new market for digital works that were previously difficult to monetise. While some celebrate NFTs as a way to empower artists and decentralise the art world, others criticise them for their environmental impact and speculative nature. Regardless of the debates, NFTs exemplify how technology continues to reshape the art world, challenging traditional notions of value and authenticity.

As these technologies converge, the boundaries between disciplines are dissolving. The next wave of creativity is increasingly interdisciplinary, drawing on art, science, technology, and philosophy to create works that defy categorisation. This convergence reflects the recursive nature of human thought, where ideas from different domains feed into one another, creating new patterns and possibilities.

At the same time, the ethical implications of these developments cannot be ignored. The power of AI, VR, and genetic engineering to create and manipulate reality raises questions about control, ownership, and responsibility. Who decides how these tools are used, and who benefits from their outputs? These questions are not only relevant to artists but to society as a whole, as creativity becomes increasingly entangled with technology and power.

The next wave of creativity also invites us to reconsider the role of the audience. As art becomes more interactive and participatory, the line between creator and consumer begins to blur. In VR installations, digital games, and collaborative projects, the audience is no longer a passive observer but an active participant, shaping the outcome of the work. This shift challenges traditional hierarchies of creativity, inviting a more democratic and inclusive approach to artistic expression.

Ultimately, the next wave of creativity is a reflection of humanity's ongoing desire to explore, experiment, and transcend boundaries. It is a testament to our capacity for innovation and our willingness to embrace the unknown. As we navigate this new era, the challenges and opportunities it presents will continue to shape not only the art we create but also the way we understand ourselves and our place in the world.

Through AI, VR, genetic engineering, and the internet, we are not just creating new tools for expression; we are redefining what it means to be creative. In doing so, we are continuing the recursive cycle of discovery and innovation that has driven human culture for centuries, opening the door to possibilities we have yet to imagine.

Chapter 16: How to Expand What We Like

Human preferences are not fixed; they are dynamic and malleable, shaped by exposure, context, and reflection. While it is natural to gravitate toward the familiar and comfortable, expanding what we like can open up new dimensions of enjoyment and understanding. Whether it is developing a taste for a challenging art form, embracing an unfamiliar cuisine, or discovering joy in a genre of music once dismissed, the process of expanding preferences is a journey of growth and transformation.

At its core, expanding preferences is about creating new associations in the brain. The mind's predictive coding system, which evaluates new stimuli against existing patterns, tends to resist what feels unfamiliar or unexpected. This initial resistance can manifest as aversion or indifference. However, with repeated exposure and the right context, the brain can integrate new patterns, transforming what once felt alien into something enjoyable.

One of the most effective ways to expand preferences is through **repeated exposure**. The mere-exposure effect demonstrates that the more often we encounter something, the more likely we are to appreciate it. This phenomenon is particularly evident in music, where a song that initially feels unfamiliar or even unpleasant can become a favourite after several listens. Each repetition allows the brain to refine its predictive models, making the experience more comfortable and rewarding.

However, exposure alone is not always sufficient. **Context** plays a crucial role in shaping how we perceive and respond to new experiences. The environment in which we encounter a stimulus can influence our emotional and cognitive engagement. For example, watching an experimental film in a lively festival setting might create positive associations that are absent when viewing it alone. Similarly, trying a challenging food in a social or celebratory context can make it more appealing, as the positive emotions of the moment influence our perception.

Social and cultural influences are particularly powerful in expanding preferences. Sharing experiences with others who appreciate something unfamiliar can provide new insights and perspectives, making the experience more meaningful. A friend who explains the nuances of jazz or a guide who contextualises an abstract painting can help bridge the gap between unfamiliarity and enjoyment. These social connections create emotional associations that reinforce the value of the new experience.

Reflection is another critical component of expanding preferences. The brain's recursive processes allow us to revisit and reinterpret past experiences, finding new layers of meaning over time. After encountering a challenging artwork, for example, reflecting on its themes, context, or techniques can deepen our understanding and appreciation. This reflective process can be facilitated by learning about the history or intent behind the work, as knowledge often enhances enjoyment.

A sense of **curiosity** is essential for expanding preferences. Curiosity drives us to explore beyond our comfort zones, seeking out new stimuli and experiences. This openness to the unfamiliar creates opportunities for growth, allowing us to discover pleasures we might otherwise miss. Cultivating curiosity can be as simple as setting an intention to try something new, whether it is attending a gallery opening, exploring a different genre of literature, or experimenting with a new recipe.

Overcoming initial resistance requires patience and an awareness of our natural biases. It is easy to dismiss something unfamiliar as "not for me," but recognising this reaction as a natural part of the brain's pattern-seeking process can help us approach new experiences with greater openness. Giving something a second or third chance, even after an initial dislike, allows the brain to re-evaluate and potentially reframe its response.

The benefits of expanding preferences go beyond personal enjoyment. By broadening our tastes, we develop greater empathy and cultural understanding. Appreciating the art, music, and traditions of different cultures fosters a deeper connection to the diversity of human experience. Similarly, exploring perspectives outside our own can challenge assumptions and enrich our worldview, making us more adaptable and resilient.

Expanding preferences also enhances creativity. Exposure to a wide range of stimuli, especially those outside our usual interests, stimulates the brain's associative networks, generating new ideas and insights. An architect inspired by abstract art or a chef influenced by global cuisines might create works that blend unexpected elements, pushing the boundaries of their field. This cross-pollination of ideas is a hallmark of innovation, driven by the willingness to explore the unfamiliar.

Practical strategies for expanding preferences include:

1. **Embracing Gradual Exposure**:
    - Start with elements that feel slightly outside your comfort zone but still have some familiarity. For example, if you enjoy classical music, explore contemporary compositions that incorporate classical elements.
2. **Seeking Guided Experiences**:
    - Engage with experts, friends, or communities who can provide context and insights. A museum tour, a cooking class, or a discussion group can make new experiences more accessible and enjoyable.
3. **Creating Positive Associations**:
    - Pair new experiences with activities or environments you already enjoy. For instance, try a new type of cuisine during a celebration or

explore an unfamiliar genre of music during a relaxing evening.
4. **Reflecting and Journaling**:
   - After encountering something new, reflect on your experience. What emotions did it evoke? What elements intrigued or challenged you? Writing down your thoughts can deepen your engagement and help you process your reactions.
5. **Practicing Patience**:
   - Give yourself time to adjust to new experiences. Tastes often evolve slowly, and initial aversions can soften with repeated exposure and reflection.

Expanding preferences is not about abandoning what we already love but about adding new dimensions to our enjoyment. It is a process that requires curiosity, openness, and a willingness to embrace the unfamiliar. By exploring beyond our immediate likes and dislikes, we enrich our lives, deepen our connections, and cultivate a greater appreciation for the world's diversity.

In the chapters ahead, we will explore how these principles apply to broader domains, from cultural exchange to personal growth, examining how the expansion of preferences shapes not only individuals but also societies. By understanding the mechanisms of preference and aversion, we can unlock new possibilities for creativity, connection, and discovery.

Chapter 17: The Role of Discovery in Shaping New Tastes

Discovery lies at the heart of human evolution, not only in the practical realms of science and technology but also in the aesthetic and emotional dimensions of life. It is through discovery, of new landscapes, ideas, tools, and perspectives, that our tastes expand and evolve. The role of discovery in shaping preferences is both profound and multi-faceted, revealing how novelty, curiosity, and exposure influence what we like and dislike.

At its most fundamental level, discovery engages the brain's reward systems, releasing dopamine and creating a sense of pleasure and motivation. This neurological response to novelty is a survival mechanism, encouraging humans to explore and adapt to new environments. In the realm of preferences, discovery provides the stimulus that disrupts familiar patterns, opening the door to new possibilities for enjoyment. Whether it is encountering an unfamiliar cuisine, a groundbreaking piece of art, or an innovative genre of music, discovery activates the mind's predictive coding system, prompting it to integrate the new with the familiar.

The relationship between discovery and preference is particularly evident in art and culture. Artistic movements often arise from moments of discovery, when new technologies, materials, or ideas disrupt established norms and inspire fresh approaches. Impressionism, for example, was shaped by the invention of portable paint tubes, which allowed artists to work outdoors and capture the fleeting effects of light and atmosphere. Similarly, the advent of digital tools has enabled artists to explore interactive and generative forms of creativity, expanding the boundaries of what art can be.

In the personal realm, discovery often begins with a spark of curiosity, a desire to explore the unknown. This curiosity drives individuals to seek out new experiences, from trying exotic foods to travelling to unfamiliar places. The process of discovery often involves stepping outside one's comfort zone, embracing the uncertainty that comes with encountering something unfamiliar. This willingness to explore is a hallmark of open-mindedness, a trait strongly associated with the expansion of tastes and preferences.

The recursive nature of the brain plays a crucial role in the process of discovery. Each new experience is mirrored and reflected upon, creating loops of reinterpretation and refinement. For instance, encountering a new style of music may initially feel disorienting or unappealing, but with repeated listening, the brain begins to recognise patterns and connections, transforming the experience into something enjoyable. This iterative process of discovery mirrors the evolution of taste on a societal scale, where once-controversial movements eventually become celebrated as mainstream.

Cultural and historical contexts also shape the role of discovery in preferences. In times of rapid change, such as the Industrial Revolution or the digital age, discovery becomes a central force in redefining societal tastes. The introduction of new technologies and ideas disrupts established norms, creating opportunities for innovation and experimentation. This dynamic is evident in movements like Futurism, which embraced the energy and speed of industrialisation, or Surrealism, which drew inspiration from the psychological discoveries of Freud and Jung.

The internet has amplified the role of discovery in shaping new tastes, providing unprecedented access to a global array of ideas, art, and experiences. Platforms like YouTube, Spotify, and Instagram allow users to explore diverse genres of music, art, and culture with just a few clicks, creating a digital landscape of endless possibilities. This ease of discovery has not only broadened individual preferences but also fostered cross-cultural exchange, exposing people to traditions and aesthetics they might never have encountered otherwise.

However, the abundance of choices in the digital age also presents challenges. The sheer volume of available content can lead to decision fatigue, making it difficult to fully engage with or appreciate new discoveries. Algorithms, designed to personalise recommendations, can create echo chambers that limit exposure to unfamiliar ideas and perspectives. Overcoming these challenges requires intentionality, a conscious effort to seek out diversity and embrace the unfamiliar.

Discovery is not only about encountering something new; it is also about deepening our understanding of what we already know. Revisiting familiar works with fresh perspectives or in new contexts can reveal layers of meaning that were previously hidden. For example, rereading a novel after a significant life event might bring new emotional resonance, while viewing a painting in a different light or setting can transform its impact. This recursive engagement with the familiar is a form of discovery in its own right, enriching our appreciation and expanding our preferences.

The transformative power of discovery extends beyond individual tastes to influence broader cultural trends. Movements like globalisation and technological innovation have created a world where discovery is a constant, reshaping tastes on a collective level. The fusion of different culinary traditions, the blending of musical genres, and the hybridisation of artistic styles all reflect the impact of discovery in creating new forms of expression and enjoyment.

At its best, discovery fosters empathy and connection, encouraging us to see the world through different lenses. By exposing ourselves to the unfamiliar, we gain a deeper appreciation for the diversity of human experience and the common threads that unite us. This openness to discovery is not only a source of personal growth but also a catalyst for creativity and innovation, as new ideas and perspectives inspire fresh approaches to art, design, and culture.

Practical strategies for embracing discovery include:

1. **Deliberate Exploration**: Set aside time to explore something entirely new, whether it is a genre of music, a type of cuisine, or an unfamiliar art form. Approach the experience with an open mind and a willingness to be surprised.
2. **Engaging with Experts**: Seek out the insights of those who are knowledgeable about the unfamiliar. A guide, mentor, or friend who is passionate about a subject can provide valuable context and deepen your understanding.
3. **Revisiting the Familiar**: Return to works or experiences you once dismissed or overlooked. With fresh eyes and new knowledge, you may discover layers of meaning that were previously hidden.
4. **Embracing Cross-Cultural Exchange**: Explore art, music, and traditions from different cultures. This exposure not only broadens your preferences but also fosters a deeper appreciation for the diversity of human expression.
5. **Allowing Time for Reflection**: After encountering something new, take time to reflect on your experience. What emotions did it evoke? What connections did you notice? Reflection helps integrate discoveries into your broader framework of understanding.

By embracing discovery as a fundamental part of life, we can expand our tastes, deepen our connections, and enrich our understanding of the world. In the chapters ahead, we will explore how these principles of discovery and preference intersect with creativity, innovation, and cultural exchange, revealing the profound ways in which new experiences shape both individuals and societies.

Chapter 18: Predicting Future Movements

Art and culture have always been shaped by the interplay of human imagination, technological innovation, and societal change. Predicting future movements requires looking at this interplay, identifying the seeds of transformation in the present, and understanding the forces that shape human creativity and preference. While the future is inherently uncertain, the patterns of history provide valuable insights into the dynamics of change, allowing us to anticipate the directions art, culture, and human expression may take.

One of the most significant forces shaping the future of art and culture is **technology**. Advances in artificial intelligence (AI), virtual and augmented reality (VR/AR), blockchain, and biotechnology are already reshaping creative processes and pushing the boundaries of what is possible. These tools enable artists to create works that are interactive, immersive, and adaptive, reflecting the complexity of the digital age. For example, generative art powered by AI algorithms allows for infinite variation and evolution, mirroring the recursive processes of human thought.

AI itself may play a central role in defining future movements, not just as a tool but as a collaborator or even an independent creator. As AI systems become more sophisticated, capable of producing music, visual art, and literature that rivals human creations, questions about authorship, originality, and authenticity will come to the forefront. Future movements may emerge as responses to these questions, exploring the relationship between human and machine creativity. Movements that challenge the boundaries of AI-generated and human-made art may spark debates reminiscent of those surrounding photography in the 19th century.

Virtual and augmented realities also promise to redefine artistic experiences. These technologies enable the creation of immersive environments where viewers can interact with or even inhabit the artwork. Unlike traditional art forms, which are static or linear, VR and AR offer multidimensional, dynamic experiences that evolve with the viewer's engagement. Future movements in this space might explore the boundaries between real and virtual, blending physical and digital elements to create hybrid realities. Entirely virtual galleries, collaborative global performances, and participatory storytelling could become the norm, inviting audiences to become co-creators.

The **internet and global connectivity** will continue to play a pivotal role in shaping future movements. Online platforms have already democratized access to art and culture, allowing creators to share their work with global audiences and collaborate across borders. This global exchange of ideas has led to the fusion of styles, genres, and traditions, creating hybrid forms that transcend cultural boundaries. Future movements may emphasise this interconnectedness, exploring themes of unity, diversity, and the blending of traditions in a globalised world.

At the same time, the digital age has introduced challenges that may inspire new artistic responses. The proliferation of social media and the dominance of algorithm-driven platforms have created echo chambers and a culture of instant gratification, where depth and nuance often take a back seat to virality. Future movements might rebel against this trend, embracing slowness, contemplation, and depth as antidotes to the fast-paced, fragmented nature of digital life. Artists may create works that demand sustained attention, encouraging audiences to reconnect with the richness of detail and the pleasure of immersive engagement.

The **climate crisis** is another force likely to shape future artistic movements. As humanity grapples with the consequences of environmental degradation, artists are increasingly turning their attention to themes of sustainability, ecology, and the interconnectedness of life. Future movements may prioritise the use of sustainable materials and processes, blending art with activism to inspire environmental awareness and action. Bio-art, which incorporates living organisms, may evolve further, exploring the relationship between humanity and the natural world in profoundly innovative ways.

Identity and inclusivity are also likely to be central themes in future movements. As societies continue to confront issues of inequality, representation, and social justice, art will reflect these struggles, amplifying voices that have historically been marginalised. Future movements may focus on intersectionality, exploring the ways in which race, gender, sexuality, and other aspects of identity intersect to shape human experience. These movements may challenge traditional hierarchies of taste and value, embracing diversity and redefining the meaning of artistic excellence.

The concept of **authenticity** will also be a significant factor in future movements. In an age of deepfakes, AI-generated content, and virtual personas, questions about what is real and authentic will take on new urgency. Movements that emphasise human touch, imperfection, and the tangible may emerge as a counterpoint to the increasingly mediated nature of modern life. These movements may celebrate the raw, the unpolished, and the deeply personal, reminding audiences of the unique qualities that define human creativity.

The role of **collective creation** is another area of potential innovation. As technology enables greater collaboration and interaction, future movements may prioritise collective, participatory art forms that blur the lines between creator and audience. Crowdsourced projects, interactive installations, and community-driven performances could become defining features of the artistic landscape, reflecting the interconnected nature of the digital age.

Finally, the **unknown**, the frontier of discovery, will continue to inspire artistic movements. Advances in space exploration, neuroscience, and quantum physics are likely to spark new ways of thinking about existence, time, and reality. These discoveries may inspire movements that explore the mysteries of consciousness, the possibilities of other dimensions, or the relationship between humanity and the cosmos.

While the specifics of future movements remain uncertain, the forces shaping them are already visible. Technology, globalisation, environmental challenges, and evolving concepts of identity and authenticity will serve as the foundation for the art and culture of tomorrow. These movements will reflect the complexities of the modern age, offering new ways of seeing, thinking, and connecting.

By looking at the patterns of history, we can anticipate that the next wave of creativity will not only build on the innovations of the present but also challenge and transform them. Art will continue to serve as a mirror of humanity, reflecting our struggles, aspirations, and boundless capacity for imagination. In doing so, it will expand the horizons of what we like, dislike, and ultimately, what we create.

Chapter 19: Designing for the Mind

Design is more than aesthetics; it is a language of communication, an interface between humans and the world. Effective design resonates with our cognitive, emotional, and physiological patterns, creating experiences that feel intuitive, engaging, and meaningful. As our understanding of the brain and body deepens, the future of design is increasingly focused on harmonising with the workings of the human mind, blending beauty, function, and psychology.

At the heart of designing for the mind is the principle of **cognitive ease**, the tendency for people to prefer things that are easy to understand and process. The brain thrives on patterns, seeking predictability and coherence in the environment. Designs that align with these patterns, whether through symmetry, repetition, or simplicity, are often perceived as more appealing. This is why minimalist aesthetics, with their clean lines and uncluttered spaces, resonate so strongly. They reduce cognitive load, allowing the brain to focus on what matters most.

However, cognitive ease must be balanced with **novelty**, which activates curiosity and engagement. A design that is too predictable risks being dismissed as dull, while one that is overly complex can overwhelm. The sweet spot lies in creating designs that offer enough familiarity to feel comfortable but introduce unexpected elements that surprise and delight. For example, the sleek simplicity of a modern smartphone interface is enhanced by subtle animations or haptic feedback that add a layer of intrigue and engagement.

Emotion is another critical factor in designing for the mind. The brain's emotional systems, governed by the amygdala and other regions, play a central role in shaping preferences. Colours, shapes, and textures can evoke powerful emotional responses, influencing how people feel about a design. Warm colours like red and yellow create a sense of energy and excitement, while cool colours like blue and green promote calm and relaxation. Curved shapes tend to feel friendly and approachable, while sharp angles convey precision and strength.

Designs that engage the **autonomic nervous system** (ANS) can create deeper, more embodied experiences. For instance, a space designed with natural materials, soft lighting, and open layouts can activate the parasympathetic system, fostering relaxation and comfort. Conversely, bold, vibrant designs with high contrast and dynamic forms can engage the sympathetic system, creating energy and focus. By understanding the interplay of these physiological responses, designers can create environments and products that align with the desired emotional outcomes.

The concept of **usability** is central to designing for the mind. A well-designed product or space should feel intuitive, requiring minimal effort to navigate or understand. This principle is exemplified in Dieter Rams' "Ten Principles for Good Design," which emphasise clarity, functionality, and simplicity. Whether it is a piece of furniture, a website, or a public space, designs that prioritise usability allow people to interact with them seamlessly, reducing frustration and enhancing satisfaction.

Digital technology has added new dimensions to the art of design, enabling interactive and adaptive experiences. Interfaces can now respond to individual preferences and behaviours, creating personalised interactions that feel tailored to each user. For example, a fitness app might adjust its interface based on a user's activity patterns, providing encouragement or suggestions at the right moments. This adaptability mirrors the brain's own recursive processes, which continuously refine and optimise responses based on feedback.

Cultural context also plays a significant role in shaping effective design. What feels intuitive or appealing in one culture may not resonate in another. For instance, colours carry different symbolic meanings across cultures; red signifies luck and prosperity in China but can evoke caution or danger in Western contexts. Designers must consider these cultural nuances, creating products and experiences that align with the values and expectations of their target audiences.

As sustainability becomes an increasingly urgent priority, design is evolving to reflect ecological concerns. **Sustainable design** focuses on minimising environmental impact, using materials and processes that are renewable, efficient, and responsible. This approach not only addresses ethical considerations but also resonates with consumers who prioritise environmental stewardship. Designs that incorporate elements of nature, such as biophilic design, can also promote well-being, tapping into humanity's innate connection to the natural world.

The integration of **neuroscience** into design is opening up new possibilities for understanding and enhancing the user experience. Advances in brain imaging and behavioural research allow designers to study how people respond to different stimuli, from the arrangement of furniture in a room to the layout of a website. These insights inform the creation of environments and products that optimise cognitive and emotional responses, whether by improving focus, reducing stress, or enhancing creativity.

Accessibility is another frontier in designing for the mind. Inclusive design ensures that products and spaces can be used by people of all abilities, creating experiences that are equitable and empowering. This involves considering factors such as visual contrast, tactile feedback, and auditory cues, as well as addressing the needs of neurodiverse individuals. By prioritising accessibility, designers create works that are not only functional but also deeply human.

Looking ahead, the future of design will likely emphasise **interactivity, adaptability, and collaboration**. Smart environments that respond to gestures, voice commands, and biometric data are already beginning to blur the lines between physical and digital spaces. Adaptive designs that learn from users' behaviours and preferences will create personalised experiences that feel intuitive and seamless. Collaborative tools will enable designers and users to co-create, fostering innovation and inclusion.

Ultimately, designing for the mind is about creating experiences that resonate on multiple levels, cognitive, emotional, and physiological. It is about understanding the intricate interplay of patterns, preferences, and perceptions that shape how people engage with the world. By aligning design with the workings of the human mind, we can create products, spaces, and systems that enhance well-being, inspire creativity, and connect us more deeply to one another and to the environments we inhabit.

This principle of alignment applies not only to individual designs but also to the larger systems in which they exist. From urban planning to user interfaces, the most successful designs are those that harmonise with the rhythms of human thought and emotion, creating a world that feels intuitive, engaging, and meaningful.

Chapter 20: Conclusion: The Recursive Muse of Humanity

Throughout history, the evolution of art, culture, and creativity has mirrored the recursive processes of the human mind. Like the brain itself, which loops through layers of sensory input, reflection, and reinterpretation, human creativity revisits, refines, and reimagines the world in an endless cycle. This interplay of discovery, invention, and preference reveals the profound interconnectedness of thought, emotion, and culture, a recursive muse that has driven humanity's most remarkable achievements.

From the Impressionists who captured the fleeting light of a rapidly industrialising world to the Surrealists who delved into the unconscious mind, each artistic movement has been both a product of its time and a harbinger of change. These movements remind us that creativity is not static; it is a dynamic process that thrives on the tension between familiarity and novelty, tradition and innovation. The brain's ability to integrate the known with the unknown is at the heart of this process, transforming aversion into appreciation and the unfamiliar into the beloved.

The journey of creativity and preference is deeply rooted in the interplay between the individual and the collective. Personal experiences, shaped by memory, emotion, and culture, give rise to unique tastes and perspectives. At the same time, collective movements and shared narratives provide the frameworks within which these preferences evolve. This duality reflects the recursive nature of humanity itself, where the individual and the communal are inseparably intertwined.

In exploring why we like what we like, we uncover not only the workings of the mind but also the forces that shape our connections to each other and to the world. Our preferences are shaped by exposure, context, and reflection, yet they are also a reflection of our identities, our histories, and our aspirations. To expand what we like is to grow, to engage with new perspectives, and to find meaning in the unfamiliar. It is an act of openness that bridges the gap between the self and the other, creating a richer, more inclusive experience of the world.

As we look to the future, the recursive muse of humanity continues to inspire new frontiers of creativity. The technologies of the digital age, artificial intelligence, virtual reality, and biotechnology, offer unprecedented tools for expression and exploration. Yet these tools also challenge us to reconsider the boundaries of creativity, authenticity, and human connection. In an age of rapid change, the question is not just what we will create, but how we will ensure that our creations remain aligned with our deepest values and aspirations.

The principles of recursion, reflection, and integration provide a guide for navigating these challenges. Just as the brain continuously refines its patterns in response to new information, humanity must remain open to adaptation and growth. This means embracing the unfamiliar, engaging with complexity, and seeking balance between tradition and innovation. It means recognising that every moment of discovery is also an opportunity for connection, a chance to see the world through new eyes and to share that vision with others.

Ultimately, the story of human creativity is a story of resilience and imagination. From the earliest cave paintings to the immersive digital landscapes of today, our ability to create has been a testament to our capacity for wonder, exploration, and transformation. It is through this recursive process of revisiting and reimagining that we find not only what we like, but also who we are.

As this book draws to a close, it is worth reflecting on the journey we have taken, from the first sparks of inspiration to the evolving frontiers of creativity. The threads that connect art, invention, and preference are not linear; they are loops of thought and emotion, endlessly intertwined. In understanding these threads, we gain insight not only into the world around us but also into the endless possibilities within ourselves.

Let this recursive muse be a reminder that creativity is not a destination but a process, a continuous unfolding that invites us to explore, to question, and to grow. Whether through the stroke of a brush, the curve of a melody, or the click of a digital tool, the act of creation is a celebration of what it means to be human: to seek, to imagine, and to share the beauty we find along the way.

Bibliography

Art History and Cultural Movements

1. Berger, John. *Ways of Seeing*. London: Penguin, 1972.
2. Gombrich, E. H. *The Story of Art*. London: Phaidon Press, 16th ed., 1995.
3. Hughes, Robert. *The Shock of the New: Art and the Century of Change*. London: Thames & Hudson, 1991.
4. Stangos, Nikos (ed.). *Concepts of Modern Art: From Fauvism to Postmodernism*. London: Thames & Hudson, 3rd ed., 1994.
5. Foster, Hal, et al. *Art Since 1900: Modernism, Antimodernism, Postmodernism*. London: Thames & Hudson, 2nd ed., 2011.

Neuroscience and Psychology of Creativity

6. Damasio, Antonio. *The Feeling of What Happens: Body and Emotion in the Making of Consciousness*. London: Vintage, 2000.
7. Ramachandran, V. S. *The Tell-Tale Brain: Unlocking the Mystery of Human Nature*. London: Windmill Books, 2011.
8. Sacks, Oliver. *Musicophilia: Tales of Music and the Brain*. New York: Vintage, 2008.
9. Zeki, Semir. *Inner Vision: An Exploration of Art and the Brain*. Oxford: Oxford University Press, 1999.
10. Kaufman, Scott Barry, and Carolyn Gregoire. *Wired to Create: Unraveling the Mysteries of the Creative Mind*. New York: TarcherPerigee, 2015.

Philosophy and Theory of Aesthetics

11. Adorno, Theodor W., and Max Horkheimer. *Dialectic of Enlightenment*. London: Verso, 1997.
12. Dewey, John. *Art as Experience*. New York: Penguin, 2005.
13. Kant, Immanuel. *Critique of Judgment*. Translated by Werner S. Pluhar. Indianapolis: Hackett Publishing, 1987.
14. Heidegger, Martin. *The Origin of the Work of Art*. In *Poetry, Language, Thought*, translated by Albert Hofstadter. New York: Harper Perennial Modern Classics, 2001.

Sociology and Cultural Studies

15. Bourdieu, Pierre. *Distinction: A Social Critique of the Judgement of Taste*. Cambridge, MA: Harvard University Press, 1984.
16. Hall, Stuart. *Cultural Representations and Signifying Practices*. London: Sage, 1997.
17. McLuhan, Marshall. *Understanding Media: The Extensions of Man*. Cambridge, MA: MIT Press, 1994.
18. Benjamin, Walter. *The Work of Art in the Age of Mechanical Reproduction*. In *Illuminations*, edited by Hannah Arendt, translated by Harry Zohn. London: Fontana Press, 1992.
19. Bauman, Zygmunt. *Liquid Modernity*. Cambridge: Polity Press, 2000.

Technology and Creativity

20. Manovich, Lev. *The Language of New Media*. Cambridge, MA: MIT Press, 2001.

21. Negroponte, Nicholas. *Being Digital*. New York: Vintage Books, 1996.
22. Ratti, Carlo, and Matthew Claudel. *The City of Tomorrow: Sensors, Networks, Hackers, and the Future of Urban Life*. New Haven: Yale University Press, 2016.
23. Anadol, Refik. *Data Paintings and Machine Learning Dreams*. Exhibition Catalogs, various dates.
24. Boden, Margaret A. *The Creative Mind: Myths and Mechanisms*. London: Routledge, 2nd ed., 2004.

The Role of Memory and Emotion

25. Tulving, Endel. *Elements of Episodic Memory*. Oxford: Clarendon Press, 1983.
26. LeDoux, Joseph. *The Emotional Brain: The Mysterious Underpinnings of Emotional Life*. London: Phoenix, 1999.
27. Proust, Marcel. *In Search of Lost Time*. Translated by C. K. Scott Moncrieff and Terence Kilmartin. London: Vintage, 1981.
28. Schacter, Daniel L. *The Seven Sins of Memory: How the Mind Forgets and Remembers*. Boston: Houghton Mifflin Harcourt, 2001.
29. Kahneman, Daniel. *Thinking, Fast and Slow*. London: Penguin, 2012.

Future of Art and Creativity

30. Kelly, Kevin. *The Inevitable: Understanding the 12 Technological Forces That Will Shape Our Future*. New York: Viking, 2016.
31. Paglen, Trevor. *Invisible Images (Your Pictures Are Looking at You)*. In *Aperture*, Winter 2016.

32. Berger, Alan. *Designing for Uncertainty: Landscape Architecture in the Age of Climate Change*. London: Routledge, 2017.
33. Harari, Yuval Noah. *Homo Deus: A Brief History of Tomorrow*. London: Harvill Secker, 2016.
34. Mitchell, William J. *Me++: The Cyborg Self and the Networked City*. Cambridge, MA: MIT Press, 2004.

Interdisciplinary References

35. Pinker, Steven. *How the Mind Works*. London: Penguin, 1999.
36. Eagleman, David. *The Brain: The Story of You*. Edinburgh: Canongate Books, 2015.
37. Csikszentmihalyi, Mihaly. *Creativity: The Psychology of Discovery and Invention*. New York: Harper Perennial, 2013.
38. Dennett, Daniel C. *Consciousness Explained*. London: Penguin, 1993.
39. Gleick, James. *Chaos: Making a New Science*. New York: Viking, 1987.

Reference

1. Adorno, T. W., & Horkheimer, M. (1997). *Dialectic of Enlightenment*. London: Verso.
2. Anadol, R. (n.d.). *Data Paintings and Machine Learning Dreams*. Exhibition Catalogs.
3. Bauman, Z. (2000). *Liquid Modernity*. Cambridge: Polity Press.
4. Benjamin, W. (1992). The Work of Art in the Age of Mechanical Reproduction. In H. Arendt (Ed.), *Illuminations* (trans. H. Zohn). London: Fontana Press.
5. Boden, M. A. (2004). *The Creative Mind: Myths and Mechanisms* (2nd ed.). London: Routledge.
6. Bourdieu, P. (1984). *Distinction: A Social Critique of the Judgement of Taste*. Cambridge, MA: Harvard University Press.
7. Csikszentmihalyi, M. (2013). *Creativity: The Psychology of Discovery and Invention*. New York: Harper Perennial.
8. Damasio, A. (2000). *The Feeling of What Happens: Body and Emotion in the Making of Consciousness*. London: Vintage.
9. Dennett, D. C. (1993). *Consciousness Explained*. London: Penguin.
10. Dewey, J. (2005). *Art as Experience*. New York: Penguin.
11. Eagleman, D. (2015). *The Brain: The Story of You*. Edinburgh: Canongate Books.
12. Foster, H., Krauss, R., Bois, Y.-A., & Buchloh, B. H. D. (2011). *Art Since 1900: Modernism, Antimodernism, Postmodernism* (2nd ed.). London: Thames & Hudson.
13. Gombrich, E. H. (1995). *The Story of Art* (16th ed.). London: Phaidon Press.
14. Harari, Y. N. (2016). *Homo Deus: A Brief History of Tomorrow*. London: Harvill Secker.
15. Heidegger, M. (2001). The Origin of the Work of Art. In A. Hofstadter (Trans.), *Poetry, Language, Thought*. New York: Harper Perennial Modern Classics.

16. Hughes, R. (1991). *The Shock of the New: Art and the Century of Change*. London: Thames & Hudson.
17. Kahneman, D. (2012). *Thinking, Fast and Slow*. London: Penguin.
18. Kant, I. (1987). *Critique of Judgment* (Trans. W. S. Pluhar). Indianapolis: Hackett Publishing.
19. Kaufman, S. B., & Gregoire, C. (2015). *Wired to Create: Unraveling the Mysteries of the Creative Mind*. New York: TarcherPerigee.
20. Kelly, K. (2016). *The Inevitable: Understanding the 12 Technological Forces That Will Shape Our Future*. New York: Viking.
21. LeDoux, J. (1999). *The Emotional Brain: The Mysterious Underpinnings of Emotional Life*. London: Phoenix.
22. Manovich, L. (2001). *The Language of New Media*. Cambridge, MA: MIT Press.
23. McLuhan, M. (1994). *Understanding Media: The Extensions of Man*. Cambridge, MA: MIT Press.
24. Mitchell, W. J. (2004). *Me++: The Cyborg Self and the Networked City*. Cambridge, MA: MIT Press.
25. Negroponte, N. (1996). *Being Digital*. New York: Vintage Books.
26. Paglen, T. (2016). *Invisible Images (Your Pictures Are Looking at You)*. In *Aperture*, Winter 2016.
27. Pinker, S. (1999). *How the Mind Works*. London: Penguin.
28. Proust, M. (1981). *In Search of Lost Time* (Trans. C. K. Scott Moncrieff & T. Kilmartin). London: Vintage.
29. Ramachandran, V. S. (2011). *The Tell-Tale Brain: Unlocking the Mystery of Human Nature*. London: Windmill Books.
30. Ratti, C., & Claudel, M. (2016). *The City of Tomorrow: Sensors, Networks, Hackers, and the Future of Urban Life*. New Haven: Yale University Press.
31. Sacks, O. (2008). *Musicophilia: Tales of Music and the Brain*. New York: Vintage.
32. Schacter, D. L. (2001). *The Seven Sins of Memory: How the Mind Forgets and Remembers*. Boston: Houghton Mifflin Harcourt.

33. Stangos, N. (Ed.). (1994). *Concepts of Modern Art: From Fauvism to Postmodernism* (3rd ed.). London: Thames & Hudson.
34. Tulving, E. (1983). *Elements of Episodic Memory*. Oxford: Clarendon Press.
35. Zeki, S. (1999). *Inner Vision: An Exploration of Art and the Brain*. Oxford: Oxford University Press.

www.ingramcontent.com/pod-product-compliance
Lightning Source LLC
Chambersburg PA
CBHW031434210526
45464CB00005B/2195